THE SCHOOL
IN THE HOME

THOMAS W. EVANS

THE SCHOOL IN THE HOME

A PRIMER FOR PARENTS OF PRESCHOOL CHILDREN BASED ON THE WORKS OF DR. A. A. BERLE, SR.

1817

Harper & Row, Publishers
New York, Evanston, San Francisco, London

FIRST EDITION

Designed by Luba Litwak

Library of Congress Cataloging in Publication Data

Evans, Thomas W.   1930–
    The school in the home.
    Based on A. A. Berle's The school in the home and Berle's self culture.
    1. Domestic education. 2. Self-culture.
I. Berle, Adolf Augustus, 1866–1960. The school in the home. II. Berle, Adolf Augustus, 1866–1960, ed. Berle's self culture. III. Title.
LC37.E85   1973   372.1'3'02813   73–4078
ISBN 0–06–011169–0

CONTENTS

FOREWORD

C. P. Snow

Tom Evans has performed a public service by resurrecting these books of Dr. Berle's. Apologetically I confess that I had never heard of them, nor of their author, though on our side of the Atlantic his son Adolf Berle, Jr. was well known. It is now clear that the senior Berle was an educator of remarkable capacity, and we might all do better if we were prepared to listen to him.

What he did was to concentrate on the intellectual and moral education (he wouldn't have believed the two could be separated) of his own children and of their friends and neighbors at a very early age: at an age where traditionally Americans haven't thought it desirable to educate their children at all, and where the English, as usual catching up with American fashion a little late, have almost left off doing so. Berle's method, carefully described, was through a process of intelligent talk, question and answer, stories and verbal play, taking up perhaps an hour or so a day, largely at mealtimes.

Berle was a Congregationalist minister, and he did his teaching with Puritan earnestness. In fact, one of the incidental charms of his work is that it incarnates the Puritan ethic at its highest, and that was one of his great strengths. But he must also have been a marvelous natural teacher and, though most educated and aspiring parents could follow his pattern, it is necessary to give a warning that not many of them would achieve his level of success.

Nevertheless, they would, if they set their minds to it, achieve some success. To an extent, not so formally or indomitably as Berle, a good many English parents in professional families have always talked something like this kind of language to their children. With many children, not with all, it works. Mr. Evans, writing with the passion of a convert and, one suspects, a fine natural teacher himself, believes that the method actually increases intelligence. Some of us would hesitate about that terminology, but it certainly could, in a good many cases, increase the ordinary measured I.Q. (I.Q. can, within limits, be coached for; this was regularly done when the Eleven Plus presided over a lot of English education.)

Mr. Evans, like Berle before him, doesn't give much weight to innate (genetic) capability. I should prefer to rephrase some of their statements. Each of us, I can't be persuaded from assuming, is born with innate limits. Just as it is unlikely that Mr. Evans or I or presumably Berle would, with our parentage, be born looking like a Japanese, it is unlikely that we should be born with the potential for hitting a baseball as hard as Hank Aaron, or doing mathematical physics with the genius of Feynman.

For each of us, some limits are laid down. The real point is that almost none of us ever reaches the full stretch which our own limits allow. That is, very few ever come near achieving their own potential, whether it is large or modest (in the technical jargon, your phenotype or mine—what we actually perform—is nothing like as grand as the genotype we were born with might have let us perform).

Even among those with obvious natural gifts, it is rare

to meet someone who has made 90 percent use of his talent.

That is why we have to work harder at education, and why I for one am interested, and more than interested, in what Berle and Mr. Evans are telling us. I should like to make one qualification on the purely intellectual side about Berle's methods. They were based largely, though not entirely, on leading children into the use of "structures"—that is, the forms in which our minds handle anything we pump into them. Fine. That was the justification for teaching the classical languages, and nowadays it is an argument for introducing "hard" languages early (German, Russian). One can perform some mental operations without having much ability in structured thought, but not many. Berle saw this very clearly. He was, one would guess, extremely good at verbal structures himself, and everything he says about the verbal aspects of education are as true today as they were sixty years ago. Academically, they are the most valuable parts of his books and show a deep insight.

Berle hadn't such an insight into his mathematics teaching. He appears to have found some difficulty with mathematics himself. He tried very hard with his children, and for workaday purposes he probably did well enough. But he wouldn't have been much help to a young child with a natural flair. Far more is now known about the teaching of the basic mathematical concepts than was available in his time. The New Mathematics has its disadvantages: it doesn't give the practice with figures that earlier generations went through: but it does give an idea of the basic structures, just as Berle's linguistic teaching gave an idea of verbal structures, and many very young children lap it up.

Not all parents will be able to use the Berle-Evans method. (I have already expressed my views on this subject in an article entitled "How 'Equal' Are We Really?," which appeared in the June 5, 1970, issue of the *Daily Telegraph Magazine.*) But the further the message is spread, the better for anyone who is capable of listening. It would certainly make for more excellence, and I would personally pay a high price if we could increase the mental excellence in our world. Let me repeat, we are very short of people who have been taught, or have otherwise managed, to make the best of their minds. If Mr. Evans were taken to heart, it could make a difference to American (or English) education before the end of this decade.

I
REDISCOVERY AND REVISION

This book teaches parents how to increase the intelligence of their children. Its methods, though simple, are revolutionary, because they demand that the most important elements of the educational process take place during the first five years of a child's life—at a time when most American children are not subjected to any systematic teaching at all. The methods suggested will be new to almost all readers. Yet they have been proved with thousands of students and in particular with one family whose remarkable story is set forth in these pages. What you are about to read is actually an important rediscovery, for the principles set out in this book were first published over fifty years ago.

In 1967 I came upon a number of musty volumes in the attic of our summer home. They were entitled *Berle's Self Culture* and were edited by one Adolf A. Berle. The series was a kind of encyclopedia for instruction of children, starting with notes on infant hygiene and proceeding through fairy tales to more sophisticated reading and instruction. Some selections were written by experts in various fields, but a number were written by Dr. Berle himself.

Although many of the selections seemed out of date and the format was somewhat old-fashioned, the books interested me because Adolf A. Berle, Jr., the author's son, had been a professor of mine at Columbia Law School. I recalled that Berle Jr. had been a child prodigy of sorts, graduating from Harvard in his teens, and that he was later a member of Franklin Roosevelt's brain trust. My personal memory of him was that he was the most stimulating teacher that I had at law school, presenting a mind both practical and far ahead of its time. Things that Professor Berle taught fifteen years ago about corporations are just now forming the basis of shareholders' actions and securities regulations about corporate management.

After reviewing *Self Culture* and using some of the author-editor's suggestions in my own home, I met with Professor Berle over lunch to see if he felt a revision and republication of his father's work would be advisable. It was clear in our conversation that he still had tremendous respect for his father and felt that the method by which he and the other Berle children had been taught was unique and productive. He suggested, however, that *Self Culture* might need mammoth revision for utilization today, while his father's basic text, a short book called *The School in the Home,* might be productively revised for current use. He told me that the methods described in the book had been developed in his home and refined with other students, over a period of some ten years, in a small school which had been set up at the Berle summer home. He also said that the book was a best seller and that thousands of parents had written his father to express appreciation for greatly enhancing the education of their children. He urged me to take a crack at revising the book and promised to send me his copy.

Teaching has always been a major interest of mine. In the course of my law practice I served on the faculty of New York Law School for a number of years and I was president of a foundation which, with a number of the country's leading universities, conducts courses and prepares materials in government for high-school teachers. I also have three young children who are eager to learn. I approached the project with enthusiasm.

Written over fifty years ago, *The School in the Home* is based on a premise which places it in the midst of the Jensenist debate currently raging in American education. The author claimed that if his method was properly used in the preschool years, a child's intelligence could actually be increased. Berle Sr. rejected the contention that genes determine genius. The results which he achieved with his students and in his family go far to support his claim.

After continued experimentation with the two Berle books in .my own home and further discussions with Professor Berle and his brother, Rudolf, I commenced the revision which is presented in these pages. I found that the two books yielded a striking and effective combination: *The School in the Home* develops a new philosophy of education; *Self Culture* is a handbook on how to implement that philosophy. Alone each represents a useful tool; together they present an entirely new system of education which can be carried out, in less than fifty minutes a day, at such occasions as mealtime, by parents in the home.

In the course of my revision, I did a great deal of research into contemporary educational literature. The record of the Berle family was convincing evidence that the method worked. I wanted to know why it worked and whether it would work today. I found significant scientific support for Dr. Berle's methods. Most of this came, however, from the bold experimenters in modern education. The methods were used in very few institutions and hardly any school systems. The scientific data which support the Berle method are set out in the last section of this book. One statement will be included here, however, because it is the very heart of the method. Muriel Beadle observes in *A Child's Mind:* "Of general intelligence (as measured at the age of seventeen, for both boys and girls) about fifty percent of the development takes place between conception and age four, about thirty percent between ages four and eight, and about twenty percent between the ages of eight and seventeen." While this statement is generally accepted by educators today, hardly anything is being done in a systematic way to use the precious preschool years in which half of a child's intelligence is developed.

In its original form *The School in the Home* was almost three hundred pages, and *Berle's Self Culture* ran to thousands of pages. Of course, the latter volumes included selections by other authors, materials that are either currently present in the average home or can be purchased without great expense. The books have been digested to the present length so that they might be used more effectively as a primer. The words are Dr. Berle's.

Two new sections have been added. A chapter entitled "The Berle Family" gives one some understanding of the remarkable results that can be achieved by the methods set forth in these pages. This is the rarest of insights, a "longitudinal study," tracing a group specially trained in childhood through their adult years. Certainly lifetime performance is the most demanding test of any educational system. The final section of this book is also new. Entitled "Berle Today," it examines the relevance of the Berle method in terms of modern educational theory. One chapter focuses on certain longitudinal studies and surveys recent scientific data supporting Berle's premise that human intelligence can be increased with proper early training. Another chapter, based on tapes of exercises with my own children and modern texts, presents ways in which the Berle method can be used in American homes today.

The author's son, Adolf A. Berle, Jr., died in 1971. In his lifetime he had been a great student, a great teacher and a doer of great things. This work is dedicated to him.

II
THE BERLE FAMILY

In 1907 Adolf A. Berle, Jr., graduated from high school and passed the entrance exams to Harvard University. He was twelve years old. He was not permitted to begin his studies at the university for two years, but after entering Harvard he proceeded rapidly to obtain his bachelor's, master's and law degrees, all *cum laude,* before he was twenty-two. He will be remembered for more than his youthful brilliance, however. Berle's life was marked by a distinguished career in law and teaching; he was an adviser to presidents, an original member of FDR's brain trust; and his writing and governmental service were directly responsible for significant changes in American law and economy.

Adolf A. Berle, Jr., had two sisters who graduated from Radcliffe in their teens and a brother who graduated from Harvard College at eighteen and received the same degrees from the university as Adolf had before him. All of the Berles went on to lead productive lives.

The Berle children arrived at their remarkable academic success, and perhaps their productive later lives, through a method of teaching devised by their father. Berle Sr. taught hundreds of children, frequently with striking success, at a school which he established at the family summer home in Boscawen, New Hampshire. Thousands of letters of appreciation from parents all over the world bore further testimony to his method, as presented in a popular book, *The School in the Home.*

Self Culture, a collection of materials to be read by and
to children, while not as popular as his other work, was
a useful guide in demonstrating how his theories could
be implemented in the home.

Adolf A. Berle, Sr., combined a number of pursuits
into a full career. For most of his life he was a Congregational minister who carried out his ministerial duties in
various pastorates and appeared in the pulpit each Sun-
day. He also served on the faculty of Tufts College,
where he was a professor of Applied Christianity. He
wrote widely, his works including two books on teaching children, an encyclopedia for use in instructing
young children and a book endorsing the Zionist position for the establishment of an independent Israel. He
frequently appeared before the Massachusetts legisla-
ture, advocating a panoply of reforms, and was adviser
to a number of public officials, including one of the better governors of Massachusetts and later senator from
that state, Winthrop Murray Crane.

Berle Sr.'s main preoccupation was with teaching
small children. *The School in the Home* was the book
which set out his theories and the way he thought they
should be applied. His methods are very much in accord
with much of modern educational theory. It is true that
in the area of discipline he does differ from many current educators in his belief in occasional use of "compulsion of the more vigorous and physical kind." But he
also knew that "it is the happiness in the children that
makes the discipline needless." Still, he was not above
giving a spanking when he thought it was needed; his
standards were high and he expected them to be followed.

Although the Berle home is described as a "school" in

the title of this book, it did not differ in outward appearance from the average New England home of its day. It was the atmosphere which prevailed in the home and the quality of the time parents and children spent together that made the great difference. As you will see from reading these pages, the quantity of time parents give their children under the Berle method does not vary markedly from the average family routine. The method involves only a few minutes each day. It must be admitted that in the Berle home both father and mother were admirably suited to the task of teaching. They divided the responsibility. Augusta Wright Berle was a talented woman, a graduate of Oberlin College who, in her late teens, had astonished her family by running off to the West to work as a missionary with the Sioux Indians. The important characteristic of the Berle parents, however, was not their intellectual or academic attainment but their attitude toward their children and their diligent pursuit of a method which made the home a place where young intellectuals could expand and develop.

Occasionally Berle Sr. wrote in a language more florid than one expects from the pen of an educator today. He was, after all, for all of his progressivism and public effectiveness, a Congregational minister writing in the 1920s. His book talks in terms of the power of doing good and evil, and he maintains that his program, if followed, will "provide a rampart against many moral wrongs." The Protestant ethic abounds and he stresses the importance of work and ambition and the elimination of waste. But if his language occasionally appears dated, the results he produced rapidly restore confidence in the efficacy of his method.

The accomplishments of the author's son, Adolf A.
Berle, Jr., both in his writings and his government service, demonstrate a brilliantly trained mind. After graduating from Harvard Law School in 1916, Berle Jr. began practicing law in the Boston law firm that had been
established by Louis Brandeis. He practiced for a year
and then joined the Army as a private. After brief non-
combatant service he became a first lieutenant and
served as a member of the Commission to Negotiate
Peace with Germany at Versailles. Because he didn't
approve of the Treaty of Versailles as it was finally
signed, he resigned from the Commission in disillusion-
ment in 1919. Looking back on this later he said, "But I
didn't lose my idealism and join the Lost Generation,
the equivalent of today's young drop-outs. I went to
work."

In the same year in which he returned from Paris,
Adolf A. Berle, Jr., set up a law practice in New York
City with his brother, Rudolf. He remained active in
this partnership for half a century, and it still exists
today. From the very beginning he devoted considerable
time to his favorite avocations of writing and teaching.
During the first two years of his practice in New York
he wrote articles on such varied topics as the League of
Nations, Santo Domingo, Haiti, Puerto Rican independence, labor power, and noncumulative preferred stock,
in such publications as *Nation, New Republic* and *Columbia Law Review.* Although his interest in international relations, with particular emphasis on Latin
America, continued throughout his life, his writings
during the twenties took on an increased emphasis in
the field of corporate law. In 1924 he became a lecturer
on corporate finance at Harvard Business School, serv-

ing in this post until 1927, when he joined the Columbia
Law School faculty.

As a young professor, Adolf A. Berle, Jr. was not content simply to turn out the usual collections of cases and
materials. His articles and books were almost always
decades ahead of their time, predicting and warning of
trends in government and economy. In 1932 he published, together with Gardiner C. Means, *The Modern
Corporation and Private Property*. (In choosing his
coauthor, Berle was also way ahead of his time. Means
was an economist and the book one of the first products
of interdisciplinary research, linking the techniques of
legal and economic analysis.) *Modern Corporation* was
epochal. Referred to even today for the proposition that
the owners of a corporation are no longer the ones who
manage its affairs, Berle and Means reviewed the areas
of stock ownership, the stock exchanges, control of
proxies and liquidity of investments, suggesting effective controls to meet the problem of absentee ownership. Other books by Berle were also prescient. Some
thirty years after the publication of his *Liquid Claims
and National Wealth*, it was used by David Bazelon in
The Paper Economy for a contemporary description of
the change in property content. A bibliography of the
published works of Adolf A. Berle, Jr. covers three and
a half single-spaced pages in the issue of the *Columbia
Law Review* dedicated to him in 1964.

Unquestionably, Adolf A. Berle, Jr. was an intellectual. But he was also a man of action. During the presi-
dential campaign of 1932 Berle, who functioned as an
adviser to candidate Franklin Roosevelt, had a bitter
argument with Professor Felix Frankfurter, whom
Roosevelt later appointed to the Supreme Court. Frank-

furter believed that big business would have to be broken into small units; Berle disagreed, maintaining that corporate responsibility could be sharpened with appropriate controls. After the campaign Berle turned down a number of more prominent offices in the administration to become counsel for the Reconstruction Finance Corporation, where he would have the opportunity to implement many of the ideas which he had developed. One by one the reforms of which he had written became part of the Federal law. Berle helped draft Section 77 B of the Federal Bankruptcy Act to liberalize receiverships, and in the course of advising President Roosevelt he suggested methods by which the Securities Exchange Act came to control stock transactions. In the chaotic days of the Depression, when drastic measures were demanded on all sides, Berle's innovative mind did much to preserve the fundamental power of the American economic system, while ensuring that the power would be used responsibly. His contribution was immense.

Dean William C. Warren of Columbia Law School has described Berle as a "scholar in politics." Again and again, in a variety of ways, Berle's hand could be seen shaping governmental events. At the same time that he was advising President Roosevelt, he was appointed chamberlain of the City of New York by Fiorello La Guardia and served in that post for four years. He took part in designing plans for the orderly growth of the City of New York. With characteristic candor he viewed the office of chamberlain as obsolete and recommended that it be abolished and its functions incorporated into other existing offices. In 1938 President Roosevelt appointed Professor Berle Assistant Secretary of State for

Latin American affairs. Serving also as a speech writer,
Berle did much to design the Roosevelt program for
Latin America and served as the President's delegate to
several Pan American conferences. In 1945, Berle
served President Truman as ambassador to Brazil. He
continued to be an effective force in the international
field throughout his life, and in 1960 President Kennedy
invited him to serve as chairman of a six-member task
force to advise on Latin American affairs. In that capacity Berle advocated creation of the Alliance for Progress. Outside of government, Professor Berle played an
active role in politics, helping to found the New York
Liberal Party and serving as its chairman from 1952 to
1955.

Adolf A. Berle, Jr. carried on a number of careers
simultaneously and enjoyed a full family life as well.
His wife is a prominent physician; they had three children, one of whom now serves in the New York legisla-
ture. Either Professor Berle's law practice or his teaching would have been enough to occupy most men. As
Justice William O. Douglas has noted, "His public con-
tributions have come in those hours when most men
turn to golf or bridge."

All of Adolf A. Berle, Sr.'s children seemed to possess
an ability and a desire for service. Although taught by
the same method, their interests differed. Lina, the
older girl, was a student of English literature, earning
her master's degree in that area, and published two volumes of literary criticism, *George Eliot and Thomas
Hardy: A Contrast* and *Comedy from Shakespeare to
Shaw.* She spoke fluent German. Her sister, Miriam,
was proficient in both Latin and French and took a
graduate degree at the Sorbonne. Both girls taught at

various schools, among them one established by their
father in New York City. As the wife of a successful
Kentucky legislator, Miriam was reasonably active in
community affairs. The youngest child, Rudolf, maintained a successful law career as partner in the firm of
Berle and Berle. His avocation was local government
service, and he was a member of the board of trustees
of his village and later a town supervisor. Interestingly,
although his brother Adolf was a Democrat and a Liberal, Rudolf was elected to office as a Republican. At the
conclusion of his local government service, Rudolf was
awarded the Scarsdale Bowl, the highest civic award in
his community.

The successful academic careers of the Berles and the
lively, practical intellects which led to such construc-
tive later lives resulted from the method of teaching
described in this book. In an era when so much of our
educational process seems geared to obtaining correct
answers on exams even though students may quickly
forget the material memorized for the test, a practice
which Berle Sr. detested, the Berle method seeks to give
the student a framework into which to place his knowledge so that he not only retains it, but uses it construc-
tively in other disciplines.

Berle Sr. referred to this goal as "mental self-organization." He describes it in this way: "Such organization
is really training in the use and application of will
power. The intellectual discoveries made through the
application of principles learned in one department of
knowledge to the problems and development of another
almost irresistibly breed a purpose to do this kind of
thing constantly and make for the growth of the will to
study, the purpose to know, the habit of inquiry or what-

ever you choose to call it, and, this established, you have again another steel girder of a mental organization in place."

Dr. Berle designed a system which creates a framework into which the young student can integrate his knowledge. It is, if you will, the thinking process, and one which its creator believed would establish a basis for judgment and taste as well as the absorption of facts. As one can see from the Berle children, the interests developed by this method varied. The system can lead to great creativity. It gives to those who master it a freedom to follow what interests them and to discern, to some extent, the substantial from the insubstantial. This method can be readily absorbed by young children and, as Dr. Berle pointed out, it should be taught, if it is to be used effectively, before the school years begin.

Perhaps because its founder emphasized the value of the Berle method to accelerate a youngster's educational program, another, and perhaps a far more important purpose, was lost sight of. That is, the Berle method can maximize one's education. By creating the initial framework, it makes the lessons of school and of life more meaningful. It does not attempt to go into the more detailed arts of teaching writing or reading to the preschool child. Instead, it develops his ability to understand and to utilize knowledge. There is much reason to believe (and this is explored at length in the last chapter) that properly applied, the Berle method can substantially increase the intelligence of young children.

So much of the education literature of today sounds of despair. Even those programs which initially appear to convey hope frequently snuff out that hope because they demand for their implementation such a large number of teachers that school systems simply cannot afford them. But the Berle method can be utilized in the home. There the ratio is always satisfactory, because the parents and the children interchangeably adopt the roles of students and teachers. There is a major place for the self-expanding intellect and self-instructing mind of the child in the Berle method. Moreover, it can be utilized, as Dr. Berle used it himself on numerous occasions, with disadvantaged children and in fatherless homes. The method increases the joy of both childhood and parenthood. It is interesting. It is fun. Its goals are to enhance the ability to enjoy, to do and to think.

III

A BERLE PRIMER

THE SCHOOL IN THE HOME

1

INTRODUCTION

This is not the work of an "educator." But that does not necessarily preclude the possibility of clearness of vision nor does it invalidate certain obvious facts of experience. Education is one of those things in which everyone has some experience and which has not been reduced to an exact science, if indeed it will ever become a science in any proper sense at all. Human life and the human mind are constantly undergoing great and fundamental changes.

For example, it is more than fifteen years since I returned from Germany, where vast changes were taking place in education. I saw individuals rise in the scale of efficiency, self-organization and self-expenditure. I saw in individuals an expansion of mental horizon which clearly showed that the juvenile mind can work under a pressure that is practically unknown here in America, without loss of strength, health or diminution of any power or physical capacity. And I saw these results in persons who could not in the slightest degree be called unusual in capability, antecedents or opportunity. I saw children not only in Germany, but in Belgium, Holland and other countries in northern Europe do an amount of work and assimilate a fund of knowledge at an early age which makes the achievements of the average school-child in America seem foolishness and waste. I resolved to try experiments in this direction myself, and for many years now, in the course of my vocation as a

preacher and pastor, I have also been teaching young
people. The results have been surprising beyond words.
These young people have responded to an intensive
treatment in instruction and guidance in a way that
shows the astonishing waste in the average American
child's life. It seems to show that while there are un-
doubted differences in children arising from their antecedents, intellectual ancestry and environment, these
are negligible in the final result if you get at the right
method, make a large enough demand, arouse the
necessary interest and exert the required force to get the
result.

The evidence of the truth of this indictment of our
public education can be had on the most casual inquiry.
Ask any well-informed parent about his children's progress in school and you will get at once a cry of discontent
and helpless protest. Such protests, in the shape of letters of inquiry about the subject matter of this book, are
in my possession by the hundreds. They come from people in all walks of life, from rich men and poor men,
from college professors to street laborers. But all these
people have one element in common. They are interested in the intellectual growth and development of
their children and are anxious to send out into the world
effective and thoroughly equipped people. Sometimes
the interest arises from the remembrance of privileges
which the parents themselves did not enjoy. Sometimes
it arises from the consciousness of the neglect of parental duty in the matter of the children's education. Sometimes it is the sincere and helpless anxiety arising from
the plain evidence, before the parents daily, that the
young people are not only not making any real progress
but are forming habits which either mean a fearful task

to overcome in the future or a hopeless handicap in the race of life. The one thing about them all is that they see with more or less clearness that the education on which we spend so much money and about which we boast so loudly and about which we are in such deadly earnest as communities and so indifferent as individuals is a fearfully wasteful and costly process.

If further testimony is necessary, ask any mature and capable teacher who has watched the progress of the public schools in the last twenty years. The teacher so addressed will tell you in plain terms that, while the teachers are doing the best they can under the circumstances, the results are steadily more discouraging. He will tell you that the capacity for steady and sustained thought on the part of the pupils seems to grow less instead of more. Rare is the community that will sustain any public superintendent or school committee in any move that will raise the standard and make the attainment of graduation more difficult. A high-school diploma may mean that the child receiving it has had some real contact with a strictly intellectual process. But for the most part it does not mean anything of the sort.

Following this line one step higher up, we come to college education. The well-known discontent now being frankly acknowledged by the presidents of all American colleges with the intellectual caliber of their graduates is the logical outcome of a process that begins in the lowest grades. The decline in respect for scholarship, especially scholarship that has nothing to do with commercial productiveness, is an effect in American life the full meaning of which many persons do not seem to comprehend very clearly. It means a lower type of civilization; it means a lower ideal of life; and it means a substantial surrender of the permanent agencies of human happiness, because it is taking out of the life of the nation the one thing which makes more for happiness than any other single element—capable self-organization. One needs only to look about and observe the vast number of persons who, reaching middle life, have no momentum in any direction. They seem to exist from day to day. They have no vital interests, no mental reserves which make it possible for them to live except by constant dynamic injections of excitement or amusement from without. Nothing shows this more than the amusements which are most flourishing. To ask a group of people to spend an evening together with only their brain power, their varied intellectual interests, to entertain them and the comparison of their aims and purposes and experiences to furnish pleasure is to risk an evening of disastrous boredom for almost everybody concerned.

In fact, this is simply the working out of the thing which has its roots far back in the earlier stages of education. The only things intensive about American life at the present moment are amusement and money-making. In these, undoubtedly, we are in fearful earnest. A baseball game is a joyous and delightsome sight, especially if it is a good game. But almost any baseball game is good enough. The reflection that thousands of people, during the most charming and delightful season of the year go, day after day, to see other people play and for hours do absolutely nothing themselves but see other people doing things is one of the most curious commentaries on contemporary American life. Now children would never do this. They want to play themselves and they do. But after they have gone through the American education mill—school, college and the rest—they are content to sit and sit, by thousands, for hours and hours and hours and do nothing but see other people play! Commercially, the same phenomenon is most conspicuous. The mad race for money, without capacity to enjoy it properly when secured, is still our outstanding characteristic.

The final result is a lower type of civilization, lessened respect for the fine and permanent things of life, an idealism that is bounded by the stock exchange or the musical comedy. The place where all this is to be combatted is in the sphere of child training, and it will be combatted by the creation of mental habits, mental outlook and mental interests that will automatically make this type of development impossible. It is in a program of intensive development for young children which will make them immune from the tendencies that not only destroy their best capacities but also make it possible for them to go through the world never knowing what they have missed and what kind of a world it actually is. There must be a mind fertilization, which is, at the same time, a sterilization against other things. There must be the arousing of interests which, by their very fire and picturesqueness and enjoyment, will make the rest seem tame and listless. There must be such a linkage of real and substantial knowledge and the process of gaining it, with delight and pleasure, as will make the senseless and idiotic things offered to rational beings for amusement seem an insult to the mind. There must be such a program and it must be begun in the home, before the school life begins, which will assimilate naturally the best things offered in the school and by natural repulsion leave the rest. There must be such a cooperation between the home and the school as will secure the continuous education of parents in the education of their children, that will make for the continuous enrichment of the intellectual life of the household and will at the same time steadily create new interests as new knowledge and new experiences are brought into the fellowship of parents and children.

Now for some concrete examples of what happened. The earliest experiments were made in my own family of four children, now aged respectively, a girl of seventeen, a boy sixteen, a girl twelve and a boy ten. At the time these plans began to go into operation the two younger children were not born, and there being but seventeen months between the two eldest, the plan admitted of treating both exactly alike. These two were admitted to Radcliffe and Harvard colleges, the girl being fifteen and the boy thirteen and a half. Their examination papers were of average or possibly slightly above average excellence, betraying nothing unusual and especially nothing that indicated "prodigies." They had simply arrived several years earlier than is usual. Two years of their college life have passed. Their standing in college is, with an occasional exception, in the honor list. Both have pursued the maximum amount of work permitted by the colleges, the boy being allowed to take six courses at Harvard, the girl only five at Radcliffe. They are in good health and nothing unusual has happened. No vital relation which ought to come with college life, associations or interests has been denied them, and they have secured all that could be expected out of their college life—in fact, rather more, as I should judge. I can see no reason for altering the course with

the two younger children, both of whom are in the Cam-
bridge High and Latin School and are beginning third-
year work. They will take college examinations and
probably be admitted at about the same ages as their
older brother and sister. There has been no crowding.
They are in absolutely perfect health judged by ordinary standards. They are not children of exceptional
ability. They have been subjects of exceptional supervision and care, both as to studies and health. If this result
had been secured with one child, the usual plea of an
"unusual child" might possibly be raised. But it is un-
thinkable that there should be four "prodigies" in one
family! The difference is one of method, parental interest and care. There have been numerous other cases
over the years of children with whom I worked in their
youth, many of whom had real problems from the
standpoint of study and, in some cases, severe physical
infirmities as well. Today these youngsters have grown
to become productive adults, with successful careers in
law, teaching and writing.

Now in all these cases there was nothing abstruse,
terrifying or otherwise beyond the reach of the average
parent. In fact, the whole thing turned upon the fidelity
of the parents, quite as much as upon that of the young
children. But even where conditions were wholly unfa-
vorable, children were enabled to do three and four
times the work, in a third or half the time usually consumed by school children. To be sure, in all these cases
a little work was kept up throughout the long vacation,
one of the absurdities of American life.

The principles which have governed in all cases were
the same. They are indicated not precisely, but generally, in the following chapters. The first thing to be

secured is the conviction on the part of parents and others who have young children in charge that there is capacity and power in the child, which only needs to be developed. Then the means by which that development can be secured must be taken. Naturally there is no arbitrary method. But the remarks made in the succeeding chapters will indicate what happened and where the line of advance starts. The parental attitude and, next to that, the teacher's attitude toward the higher things of the mind is of paramount importance especially in young children.

The often contemptuous indifference with which mature people treat the presence of children in their habits, manners and conversation is to me one of the paralyzing wonders of contemporary life. This is especially observable in matters of speech and the use of the mother tongue.

2

LANGUAGE, THE INSTRUMENT OF KNOWLEDGE

Language is the tool by which all knowledge is acquired. There are persons who can make themselves understood and can convey ideas by signs and motions of various kinds, but the usual medium for conveying ideas is language. The earliest form in which language begins to assert its influence upon the human mind is in the spoken tongue. It is hardly an accident that we speak of the "mother" tongue. It is in the home that the most durable habits of speech are acquired, and, generally speaking, it is in the home that whatever style develops in mature life has its origin. The proper vocalization of words has an effect upon children which is often overlooked. Almost everybody is fond of repeating the baby's efforts to talk, and "baby talk" lingers in many homes— an innocent but costly pleasure for the parents and the children alike. There are many persons of mature age at this moment who will never pronounce certain words properly since they became accustomed to a false pronunciation in childhood because somebody thought it was "cute." There are many persons who will never get over certain false associations of ideas because somebody thought it was very amusing and funny to see the child mixing up things in such a beautifully childlike way!

Let me call attention to a contrast at this point which

may suggest what this particular chapter has to explain. What parent, if he discovered some physical disability in the speech of a young child which meant imperfect vocalization, like lisping, for example, or stuttering, would not make haste to employ every possible means to secure the early correction of the evil? Or again, suppose some father discovered that his child had a malformation of one or both feet, which meant, if unattended to, that the child would never walk straight or stand erect? Can we imagine that this defect would be ignored, glossed over and forgotten simply because for the moment it caused no discomfort or involved no pain?

Pass now from the region of physical development into the region of the mental life, and contrast the method of procedure. A child makes, through undeveloped organs, some funny mistake in the vocalization of a word. Everybody laughs and the child is promptly encouraged to make the same mistake over again. Not only is the child deceived as to the fact concerning that particular thing, but its ears are misled at the same time, interpreting the sound it heard as a correct one and therefore to be repeated in that connection. There was integrated into the mind of the child an error which either had to remain there or later be expelled by a special process.

From the earliest moment we seem to make every provision possible for perfection of the physical structure in which the mind operates and carelessly leave, till we are forced to deal with it, the habits and activities of the mind itself. "But what do you want me to do with my baby?" says some irate man who thinks I am going to demand a philosophical thesis from the baby in its cradle. This is what I want him to do: If he sees a defective eye I want him to get it mended. If he sees a defective word I want that mended, too. When one of my own children was small I noticed a certain tendency to make bad work of a certain combination of consonants. Thereafter daily for several weeks, as a playful exercise with this baby, I repeated in his ear the proper vocalization of that combination, and presently the confusion disappeared. Left alone, that habit would have become fixed. It would have affected the spelling of that particular combination as it appeared in words. It would have confused the eye every time it saw them, because it would have been inharmonious with the sound which lingered in the ears and which had been made domiciliary in the tongue. That slight defect might have operated for confusion, for distress and for blunder in a hundred different ways of which I do not even know. But by simply whispering into the baby's ear daily, as a matter of playful intercourse, the thing was eliminated. Apply that principle to the use of words. Apply it to habits of correct speech and the use and power of approach to the mother tongue in the ordinary child in the first three or four years of life and it will produce something which will seem like a dream. This training begins not with the child but with the person or persons who have the child in charge. In general, it means the parents.

Language, as I have said, is the tool of knowledge. It is the instrument by which we gain and garner information, by which we coordinate what we know and make inferences and express results. But if you blunt the tool, not to say destroy it, before you begin to use it, how are you ever to get knowledge in any proper or real sense? Everything depends upon this tool. The mastery

of a proper use of the mother tongue is the first and last
requisite of sound and extensive mental development.
Language is the key to everything that pertains to human life. Once get a language and you have the key to
manners, civilization, habits, customs, history and all
the complex and fascinating story of humanity. That
process begins almost at the cradle. It begins by cul-
tivating accuracy and skill in the use of the tongue. It
begins by striking at and out every false thing, the moment it appears.

One of the things that interested me greatly in the
Low Countries was the facility with which children
spoke four or five languages. Of course, in the Low
Countries the intermixture of nationalities makes it absolutely necessary for every child to master several languages in order to do business with the contemporary
life around him. But what struck me most was that the
cross-fertilization of thought produced by this interlin-
gual development was even more important than the
thing itself. It convinced me that linguistic study has in
it more power for the development of mental force and
freedom than any other kind of study. It convinced me
that the decline in America of the classics, Greek and
Latin, on the score that they were not "practical" is a
species of foolishness which some day we shall greatly
deplore.

The use of the mother tongue is the most important
factor of the whole educational process. It is the means
by which entrance is made into the vast world of books.
Once that world is entered, the novice knowing his tool
and having the tool properly edged and sharpened, he
is brought at once into contact, possible in no other way,
with the vast stores of knowledge. And observe, when

you have trained a child in good English and prevented him from learning a great mass of bad English, when you have spent his earliest years familiarizing him with a correct and extensive vocabulary, you have given him access to a great many things from which the other process automatically excludes him. Now there are great treasures in the libraries which even young children would enjoy if they only had the tool by which they could use them. But their "club" minds having been neglected, having been encouraged because it was "cute" and "pretty," they are automatically excluded from this world. That means the delimitation of their activities almost from the start. Sometimes it means a permanent exclusion from some of the choicest delights of life, for taste, like everything else, develops early, and taste in literature and knowledge and things intellectual requires very careful and exacting attention in the early stages. Who does not recall the hatred for some branches which was bred in him by the stupid, blundering person who was their titular representative? I had myself exactly this experience with mathematics, until I struck a fascinating creature who made geometry seem like poetry and who talked about algebra as though he were describing foreign travel! The same thing can be done with almost any branch of knowledge, if there is the skill, the zest and the industry and the love of it to do it. It can be generated in almost any child for almost any subject.

Now this is in no wise a technical or involved matter at all. It requires on the part of parents and teachers and the custodians of young life generally interest and care in watching the process of the formation of the habits of speech and the use of words. It requires that the per-

sons named shall themselves keep correct habits in the
presence of their children. It demands that when an
error appears, it shall promptly be supplanted by the
corresponding correct usage. In practice this will be
found to be really a very enjoyable process. There is
hardly any pleasure comparable to the pleasure of seeing the mind of a child grow. And there is a special
pleasure in seeing it grow beautifully and develop satisfactorily in every respect. Perhaps the most outstanding
and interesting manifestation of such sound growth and
development is the evidence that ideas are coming into
existence naturally and accurately. One who does these
things will have the same sensations, only much more
delightful, in hearing his child speak a difficult word
properly that he has when the child walks across the
room the first time without assistance.

No instrument tends to clarify thought as much as a
keen linguistic sense. By its very nature it creates shad-
ings and attitudes and perceptions which operate for
the sharpening of the mind to distinctions; and what is
clearness of thought but the ability to make accurate
distinctions readily and habitually? Permanent defects
are bred in childhood. The tongue, the eye and the ear,
instead of being promptly set to work together by constant correction, through good usage and by the elimination of errors, get out of the habit of working together.
Often the eye deceives the ear, and not infrequently the
tongue deceives the other two. What linguistic development does in early youth is bring about this coordination and working together; the three make a wonderful
combination for thought and for the acquisition of
knowledge.

Verbal analysis is another thing which may be begun

in the linguistic training of children at a very early
period. Many of my readers, probably most of them, are
familiar with Kingsley's *Water Babies*. Very likely,
many who read that fascinating and charming child's
book to their children, when they come to the chapter
which deals with the professor's ailment, with Bump-
sterhausen's blue follicles and the doctors' diagnosis of
his case, skip over those long words, medical, surgical
and otherwise, which make that chapter such a linguistic delight. But I found that the reading of those chapters carefully and with strict and precise enunciation
bred in my own children a great delight and amusement
in the effort to repeat them. I attribute to that book and
that particular chapter a great deal of influence in my
own household in the development of a resource of
vocabulary which has been almost priceless in their
education. Remember that every four- or five-syllabled
word generally has a history. That history is itself a
"story" for children *par excellence* if properly told and
interestingly set forth. And, be it also remembered that
polysyllabic words are usually composed of simple
words and may be taken apart, just exactly as a child
takes off the arms and legs of a doll and digs out the
stuffing to see what it is made of. Why should a child
that can say *cat, a* and *log* not say *catalogue?* As "stories" for children, the history of many long words is as
fascinating as anything possibly can be. And all the
while you are training the ear for linguistic changes,
you are taking language apart and showing how it is put
together. You are really teaching verbal analysis, which
is itself a very scientific process and one of the best for
the development of the mind and the cultivation of
ready and clear speech. Anybody who has access to a

dictionary can do this. And many parents will add to
their own store of information by so doing and will gain
pleasure for themselves and their children. This will
make a bond of union on the mental side, which is quite
as interesting and quite as desirable for the uses of life
as the physical bond.

This is really nothing more than what is habitually
done in other things. We often tear a flower apart and
show its structure to children that they may see how it
grows and where its life resides. We often take insects
and have children watch them to see how they work and
how they are able to perform what they do. Why not take
words apart and make language interesting in exactly
the same way? I can hear some man say to me at once,
"But I am not a philologist." Nobody asks you to be a
philologist. It is only needful to take a dictionary and
utilize what you have and break it up into digestible
fragments for the child. I have heard many children ask
their parents what certain long words meant because
they struck the ear musically or curiously. But I have
rarely seen the parent that would stop instantly and tell
all that she could tell about that word, thus utilizing the
interest which was there ready to be stimulated and
enriched by further knowledge. But I have often seen a
mother break into a sentence and give a child's hair
ribbons the proper twist so that they might look right!

Now, as it happens, the English tongue is allied to
many other languages. And there is hardly a city in
America where the opportunities for observation in the
comparison of languages is not afforded on streetcars
and in public places. Children, if they are trained to it
and directed to it, make most admirable use of their
opportunities in this respect to their vast enjoyment.

There creeps into casual intercourse a great mass of words which in their superficial resemblance to English words make opportunities for word "stories" and open the way for imparting a great deal of collateral information, in the way of fertilization, of which I shall speak in a later chapter.

All thinking is in terms of language, and until there is a sound linguistic basis you can have no real thinking. It is, therefore, the paramount problem of education to create first and foremost in the minds of young children as rich and full and varied a knowledge of words as possible. It is not necessary that they shall fully "understand" all that these words mean or all that can be made of them. It is enough that what they do know is accurate and is not allied to something that is false and that requires to be unlearned. The supposition that this initial contact with the mother tongue must be always in the simplest and most elementary forms is, in my judgment and according to my experience, wrong. Composite sounds and the most varied syllabic construction can be taught with very little effort, and, if allied to the most simple musical knowledge and made rhythmic, there is almost no limit to what can be done. I have taught a child to repeat an entire Hebrew psalm, with absolutely not a single error in pronunciation, without the child's "understanding" anything about it other than that it was the Hebrew way of saying what the child knew in English and had learned as a part of his Bible study. I have taught a child to repeat fifty lines of Virgil in exactly the same way. Of course somebody will say, "What was the use?" The use was, apart from the fact that it created traditions and mind stuff, that it taught careful vocalization and trained the ear to note the varied

succession of sounds and established the ability to grap-
ple with any word, however long or however unfamil-
iar. What is this but the process reduced to a program
which we employ casually and in a slovenly manner
when we simply let children learn their mother tongue
by hearing it talked? This is simply organizing the
materials out of which the linguistic consciousness
shall be made. It is the erection of barriers against
misuse and defective usage. It is the building of the solid
substructure of knowledge by the formation of standards which once made have a determinative influence
in the whole subsequent contact with the things for
which language is employed. It means that certain
things are automatically excluded and made impossible
in the educational development of the child mind. It
means that all along the pathway of its growth it will
find materials planted in the early years which will be
lights for illumination of dark places and guides for the
pathway out of obscurity and mental confusion. Many
things not "understood" by a child are nevertheless, I
have found out, stored away in the mind and, at the
appropriate moment, reappear to give the pleasure and
delight of the renewal of an old acquaintance. The child
that has built up for it a sound and considerable and
varied vocabulary before it is six years of age will have,
other things being equal, three years' start on any child
not so trained. It will have access to more books, more
forms of knowledge, will have intellectual interests and
intellectual enjoyments that the average child of nine
not only does not know but in many cases probably
never will know. I count this linguistic training as the
most important factor in the whole scheme of intensive
development for children. I cannot see that the child

loses one thing that it would otherwise have. I cannot see that any child pleasure, any child enjoyment, any rational and sound and delightful characteristic of true and happy childhood need be interfered with in the slightest. But on the contrary I have seen childhood develop and its companionship and fellowship with parents, with nature, with the world, with the phenomena of life vastly increased and happy childhood made happier because there were left no cruel malformations to cause the heartbreaking distresses of later school years.

3

MIND FERTILIZATION

Some years ago, having recently moved into the country, I noted how a certain neighbor of mine, who had been very successful in raising apples, prepared the soil for some young trees he was setting out. He did not simply dig a hole and stick in the trees. He carefully studied the nature of the soil, the requirements of the particular trees he was planting, provided for their growth in their earlier years, and in every manner possible saw to it that his trees should come to the bearing period strong, healthy and thoroughly fitted to make the greatest possible yield. He and his farm are in distinct contrast to all those around him. The others rarely yield any profit; his always yields a profit. The children on those other farms, as soon as they were able to work, left school and joined their careless, untrained parents in making a bare living from the land. His children, as they have come along, have gone to fitting schools and colleges. He ships apples to Europe, lives well, is a reading man, has a lovely home and otherwise makes his New Hampshire place furnish not only a living but a life. Reduced to lowest terms, it comes of the fact that he fertilizes the soil for the trees which furnish the income out of which all his other enjoyments and advantages arise.

It is one of the anomalies of our time that this perfectly simple and natural process is so little applied to children. Take almost any community in this land and you will be surprised to find that there is an almost complete absence of plan in the matter of stocking the child mind with useful, fertile notions and a neglect of the mental soil, which, in any other operation, would be pronounced scandalous in the extreme.

How many persons systematically think of giving to the growing mind the raw materials of knowledge and the elementary forms of science and generally of habituating the minds of children to grasp important and useful facts and otherwise prepare for some adequate familiarity in mature life with the world in which they are to live and move and have their being? How many, even of educated parents, have a clearly thought-out plan for filling the minds of their children with the things without which successful access to mental fullness and enjoyment is well-nigh impossible? In other words, who thinks of doing for the child mind what my friend the farmer does for every tree he plants?

One reason why so few people think along these lines is the prevalence of the superstition that the child mind cannot grasp important and fundamental things as readily as foolish and absurd things. Hence the "simplification" of all sorts of things for the child mind and the reduction to something worse than folly of the operations of the young intellect on the theory that whatever ideas are given to it have to be made semi-idiotic before the young intellect can handle them.

Why should the baby be filled with carefully selected nutriment for his little body and then stuffed with all sorts of rubbish for his little mind? The object of this chapter is to convince and persuade you that if you want your child to have a full mind and a well-nurtured one, you must fertilize it, so that when ideas present themselves, they will find a soil fitted to receive them. This means that you regulate not only what ideas are received but also when and in what form, that there shall be an intelligent and deliberate choice of ideas for the child mind and, most of all, that what goes into the mind shall have some relation to the higher views of life; and that mental weeds shall not possess the soil to such an extent that half of life has to be consumed in rooting out what has been by neglect and blunder permitted to occupy the soil.

Among the very first things to consider in this relation is that among what are called the higher things of life, the more profound are as easily acquired in childhood as any others. A child can be taught the fundamental principles of geometry, for example, at three as readily as he can be taught to build a block house. He can be taught to observe relations which are fundamental mathematical calculation as easily at four as he can any of the nonsense which is usually supposed to be fit for children at that age. Even the fundamental principles of philology can be thus taught, and I have seen children at three, four and five analyze words and recognize stems and make proper and cogent inferences by reason of resemblance in form and use. Of course, somebody had to call the child's attention to these things. I recall well dealing with a very young child once on the subject of *species.* This is a scientific word and involved considerable explanation, but it was worth all it cost in both time and effort when after a rain the little girl, seeing a robin pick up a worm, propounded the question, "Papa, fishes eat worms and birds eat worms. Do they belong to the same *species?*" To rouse that mental operation was itself to start the sources of knowledge from their hiding places. The worms in question brought forth another interesting specimen of the automatic application of the child mind to questions of knowledge. The small boy aged four, being told about worms being articulates and the possibility of the growth of their various segments, was found on the same occasion that the "species" episode occurred cutting up worms into parts, with a view to multiplying the species, having also been told that they kept the soil loose so that the plants could spread their roots more readily in the loosened soil. There you had one of the great scientific generalizations, one of the great geological facts of the distribution of the earth's surface, properly and firmly habited in the child's mind in a fashion which need never be disturbed.

In a similar way the silver at the table, the glass, the china, the food and its sources all become the media for the conveying of exact and interesting knowledge. Now the important idea about all these things was not merely that real and useful information was placed in the mind, but that the mind itself was being fertilized for the subsequent reception of other information and provided with the machinery for its proper classification and retention. In this way geography and arithmetic and grammar and various sciences were taught, not as such, but as fertilizing material which by their occupancy of the mind excluded the vile stuff which is usually doled out to the infant intellect. What is more, and perhaps best of all, was that these particular children were made immune from the misuse of their minds later on in life. There was nothing supernatural about it. It was simply doing what my friend the farmer did for his trees. The mental soil was fertilized by things inherently useful, interesting and suggestive, and a rudimentary organization was set up to properly husband what came into the mind for future use.

The fertilization here described was of course of the nature of the surroundings of the children in question. A legal friend of mine who was accustomed to take home with him cases to prepare for trial was greatly astounded after several months to hear his young son, who often sat in the next room while he was dictating to his stenographer, not merely use but accurately apply many legal terms in his play. He heard his small boy repeat the most complicated legal sentences, those remnants of barbarism, the rage and despair of all lovers of truth and justice and the proper use of language. He heard this child utter with ease and skill whole paragraphs of pleadings and was both shocked and humiliated to find that his child, left to himself, grappled with the severities of the language under their most grotesque and damnable forms (no other word fits the legal nomenclature) while he habitually talked twaddle and foolishness with his child. A physician classmate of mine related something of the same sort about one of his children, who learned to connect certain ailments with certain symptoms and diseases and who often made the physician feel absolutely silly when he wrote a prescription, remembering the comments of his child upon the same diseases. But why need he have been surprised? The child mind will take what is offered. Offer it falderal and idiotic stuff in the shape of brutalized English and misinformation of all kinds and that will be its mental subsoil. Offer it knowledge—clear, accurate and classified—and you will get an orderly mind and one that governs and regulates its own processes presently. Nor will this little mind be a genius! It will simply be as well fed in mind as it is in body. It will simply have as much attention given to what it thinks as to what it eats. In other words, parents will be thinking almost as much of the brains of their children as they now think of their bowels. Is it so revolutionary a principle as some people seem to imagine that you get out of a child's mind what you put into it?

The objection most commonly urged against this process of enriching the minds of children by real knowledge and worthwhile material is that it interferes with the child's healthful growth and development. This seems one of the most foolish ideas that ever obsessed the human brain. But the answer to this objection is simply that it is not true. Not a single reason can be adduced to show that giving a child information about geometry is one whit more calculated to break down health than to give it Mother Goose rhymes. Nor can it be shown that to give it accurate knowledge about botany is one degree worse for its physical well-being than to chatter simply about the "pretty flowers." Some kind of information the child is bound to gather. Some kind of ideas is sure to germinate and occupy the soil. If nonsense, then you have a nonsense foundation, which will assuredly have to be forked over and dug out as a garden has to be forked to get out the weeds if you are to have productiveness afterward.

When the fertilizing process has been carried on for a few years, one sees just what takes place in a carefully planted orchard or a carefully arranged garden, each thing in its place, each healthily developing, each bearing in its season after its own kind and each supplementing the other in beautiful cooperation and correlation. I am at this moment thinking of the great natural processes which were taught to little children, not far from the place where this is written, by watching the operation of ants, bees, wasps and birds; of the biological principles which were here shown and steadily developed so that when the same children who "played" at knowledge with these found themselves face to face with the "science" of the same things in college, they met old friends with delight. If anything was done in the matter of the beauty and innocence of childhood, it was extended and given a longer lease on life and a continuity into the severer questions of maturity, which made the natural difficulty of these problems somewhat less, because they seemed interwoven with the development of life itself, as indeed they are. The incomparable folly of postponing the period of knowledge till it has to be approached with perverted tastes and muddled ideas is equaled only by the insanity that this process conserves the beauty of childhood.

Clearly this is a parental question. It cannot be left until the period called "school age," as though this age came automatically according to some heavenly arranged arithmetical succession. By the time what is called school age arrives, the damage has usually been done. The habits, while not utterly deranged, have been deformed by ill usage and the very mind stuff itself corrupted by the infusion of all kinds of superstition, puerility and falsehood, so that only the most persistent effort on the part of everybody concerned—parent, teacher, and the whole organization of church and state and home—can scarcely bring order out of the chaos which the early sterilization of the mind has produced.

But just gaze for a moment on the reverse of the picture I have presented. Here is born a child into a home where from the moment of its appearance, yes, long before its appearance, there is preparation made for the little stranger's mind as well as his body. Along with the little bassinet which contains the covering for his body, there is a well-defined program for his mind. There is an arrangement of what his eyes shall look upon, what his ears shall hear and the form and methods by which the earliest ideas shall find their way into his mind. He shall be taught the truth. That guarantees his freedom! He shall be given useful and interesting knowledge of real life. That ensures reality for him in the outer world. He shall be trained to see with his eyes and hear with his ears, and he shall be shown how to coordinate what enters through these two gates to his mind. That will give him tools for his mind and thoughts for his tongue. He shall speak, when he speaks at all, accurately, and his linguistic machinery shall from the very first help him, not hinder him. He shall learn to note sounds and distinguish sweet sounds from those that are harsh. He shall try his mind as he tries his little arms and legs and shall gain mental strength coordinately with his physical growth so that while he walks on his legs, he shall not creep in his mind. He shall have his mind food as carefully chosen as his bodily food, and he shall be kept mentally true and clean as he is cleansed daily and bathed bodily. Is the result hard to imagine? Not at all. This child will be original, will be fearless, will have the power and the interest of experimentation, will show zest for all kinds of knowledge, and will find the gathering of information as great a joy as he can possibly know. Presently somebody will call him a "prodigy," absolutely ignorant of the simple and entirely natural

process by which the all-round development of the child
has been secured. And possibly another person will
want his progress "retarded" lest he become "prematurely old" and "lose his youth," and Heaven knows
what other folly will be foisted upon him simply because his mind was properly cared for as my old farmer
friend prepared the soil for his tree. The tree was
planted in good ground and it brought forth abundantly.
That was all!

4

QUESTIONS AND ANSWERS

There is no surer method of determining real progress in any direction than the effective use of question and answer. The Socratic method—telling things by being asked about them or creating the materials of thought by arousing questions in the student mind and then causing the inquirer to answer his own questions —remains still the best method of producing sound mental action and steady mental force.

Questions have several characteristics which are not commonly appreciated as having very important influence in the child mind. A question rightly put is an exchange of ideas between two living personalities who are not merely searching for knowledge but are comparing ideas. This is what constitutes the chief difference between a question in a book and an oral question. No inquiries printed on a page of a book will ever elicit what the same questions will secure when verbally addressed from one mind to another. Manner, intonation, accent, the glance of the eye and a great many other things which are absent from the printed page accompany the oral question. Then again, the flexibility of language often admits two or even more interpretations of exactly the same words. That admits at once doubt, which is itself the greatest thought-disperser I know anything about. Only create hesitation about the meaning of a printed question and you have taken a most substantial step toward making it impossible for a child to organize his thoughts on that particular subject. This is the reason why teachers are so often mystified by the differences between the apparent attainments of a child in class and his utter failure to make the same impression when confronted by an examination paper. And until examination papers are written in a form which does not admit of ambiguity, and few papers can be written which will not admit of a variety of interpretations, this difference will always appear.

This is not confined to children and the student body alone. It has taken the Supreme Court of the United States twenty years to find out just what the law relating to huge industrial combinations means. Turn a moment to another profession. All successful medical practice turns upon successful diagnosis. But what are the facts when you have a serious case of sickness? Not infrequently the very best minds will give totally different interpretations of exactly the same data. Why should a child be expected to find from a printed question the exact reply which was in the teacher's mind in framing the question?

Questioning is an art. That must be recognized first of all. And as an art it must be cultivated. There is nothing particularly mysterious or baffling about it. In a similar way replying is also an art and may be cultivated, and there is nothing mysterious about that. And where the relations of the questioner and the questioned are sound relations, art will develop naturally and will prove to be one of the most fertile instruments of mental development. The true manner of discovering whether certain knowledge has been mastered and is a permanent part of the mental furniture or not turns very largely upon this item of questions and answers. To frame a question properly constitutes the fine art of teaching. And to begin the framing of questions properly with little children is to prepare them for giant strides in intellectual advancement. Who ever thinks of putting questions to little children with exactness and with the purpose of causing exact mental effort on the part of the child?

From all this I wish simply to establish the extreme importance of the personal equation in the matter of giving and extracting knowledge. My point is that this process should begin so early that the necessary allowances in a child's mind will be made and such judgment developed and exercised that the almost necessary ambiguity, inherent in a language like the English language, will be met by the ability to think around the subject and make some just and correct inferences as to what the question probably means. This involves the cultivation in the home of the art of questioning and of answering questions and of interlinking factual knowledge with inferential judgments so as to make available whatever knowledge there is in the child mind.

The earliest years of life are the ones in which the mind is most eager and in which the inquiries come with least artificiality and with the greatest directness. This is the time to answer with the most abundant information, with the largest relationships and with the widest possible collaboration. For example, there is a war in progress and the names of places and the civilization of the contending nations are discussed at the breakfast table. That is the time to answer the child's question with the greatest possible fullness. It is a time not merely to answer with clearness and precision the thing called for, but to link it with the great variety of collateral things which are at that moment so related to the question asked as to enable the parent to teach simultaneously history, geography, manners, morals, language, philology and much more besides. Here again the outcry will be at once, "Oh, but we have not the equipment to do all this." My reply is that this is nonsense, for even the daily newspapers, the best of them, do this very thing, and it involves in its least capable form merely the intelligent gathering of special news articles and the careful reading of them, the intelligent and careful scrutiny of a map and a walk to even the most meagerly equipped town library and the examination of the catalogue for a book or two on the subject. All this should come out of a question brought forward under the circumstances indicated. The same thing is true concerning inventions or great events and is specially true concerning great personalities.

With little children the most trivial things can be linked with solid knowledge so that the results are almost beyond belief. Nor must all this be supposed to lead to, or necessarily involve, undue or unpleasant maturity on the part of the child. Any information which comes in a natural way is interesting and has the accompaniments which make it possible to be linked with what is already in the child's mind. The fact that a child asks, "What kind of people are the Turks?" makes the natural background for finding out what induced that question and then putting in with strong and sumptuous liberality the background which will make that question, when asked again, luminous with many kinds of replies. To tell what kind of people the Turks are gives the natural opportunity for teaching history, for recalling inspiring romance, for dealing with fundamental questions of morality and religion—the foundation problems of civilization and humanity. Why should it be postponed?

The psychology of this matter of questioning is most interesting. A child's question is really an exhibit of its method and premier interests. When young children question, you have generally a simple idea, and while it is in itself a simple idea, its form almost always reveals the general notions and leading thoughts out of which it has come. When a child asks a perfectly stupid question, one which does not readily indicate out of what mental movements it arose or what soil generated it, there is the very best of reasons for going at once into the business of finding out what is the matter with his fundamental mental operations, because children do not usually ask stupid questions. Sheer and absolute ignorance does not ask stupid questions. Absolute innocence asks the most direct questions possible without fear and without shame. Stupidity arises from confusion of ideas. And if this confusion is met with more confusion, you simply pile up trouble for the later years of the student life. Such a situation should be met with intelligent questioning as to whence the original question, how induced, with what interest in mind, and, in fact, the bringing out of the entire mental furniture of the child into the open so that what is rubbish will readily reveal itself. Not to do this is to add to every subsequent handling of the theme elements that cannot possibly do otherwise than destroy clearness in thought or successful handling of knowledge gained.

The fact is that questions and answers assume that the people asking and the people answering live within mental speaking distance of each other. The important thing is to get the mental touch which links the question

to the interest, the personality of the child, and which
admits of the utilization of previous knowledge and inquiry. Nowhere can this situation be secured with such
perfection of detail, with such satisfactory and suggestive surroundings, as in the home. The natural affections, the habitual association of ideas, all tend to make
an adequate and satisfactory framework for both the
question and answer. And the comparison of question
and answer instantly opens other avenues of information, and few occasions of such intercourse stop with a
single question. One thing leads to another and, before
that question is disposed of, many other things have
been opened for inspection, more and other questions
have been raised and the foundation has been laid for
a resumption of the instruction at another time. There
is another rather important distinction between questioning at school and questioning at home, the influence
of which is significant in the development of a child's
mental life. Answering at school contemplates as a rule
simple accuracy—satisfaction of the supposed desire of
the instructor. But questioning in the home takes on the
aspect of a search for truth as distinguished from mere
accuracy. It is not unknown both in school and college
for young people to come to understand that this or that
teacher requires certain replies to certain questions. Indeed many such "standard" answers are handed down
from one class to another. But this is not the case when
it comes to the interplay of the parental and the filial
mind. Here the subject is up because of its intrinsic
interest to one or the other party to the interrogatory. If
it begins with the child, the parent, by reason of interest
in the advancement of the child's knowledge and culture, will make the most of the opportunity to give much

information and give it with reference to the total life of the child and especially as a veracious foundation for judgment, for comparison and future light. Mere correctness gives place to a larger ideal of the matter in hand. If it originates with the parent, the child will naturally also presume that the subject itself is invested with importance and interest utterly apart from his ability or inability to furnish a correct answer. This creates a totally different situation and one in which the rational search for truth is begun and which, persisted in, creates a habit of intellectual veracity that is as important an adjunct to the intellectual life as knowledge itself—perhaps even more important. And it comes into the child's life associated with parental authority and habit, which is best of all.

The art of answering questions is one which in cultivation has a decisive influence in training the young mind to seek out the essential from the trivial or unessential elements of any given subject. Nothing makes a young mind glow with enthusiasm like the experience of seeing that a simple question has loosed a great stream of information and produced what the inquirer did not dream was involved when he spoke. Tapping a full mind is an exercise which yields great satisfaction both ways. For children it is a perennial source of delight and, once they experience it, they will come back again and again with questions, if only for the pleasure of seeing what their questions will bring forth. Now out of this fullness there is a choice to be made. The wise and observant parent will make rapid analysis of what associations have brought out the question. He will select a few leading or striking things in connection with it and will leave certain determinative marks upon the

mind around which the less important details will
readily group themselves. This is an easy enough process to the mature mind, but not so easy for the young.
But seeing the thing done often and seeing discrimina-
tion made, the child soon learns the habit of discrim-
ination and begins to imitate the phrases, the attitudes
of mind and the expressions by which the choices are
indicated.

Little children especially are fond of recitals of personal experience and, properly guided, offer beautiful
narratives which are the most natural material one
could desire for training of the mind. I have known of
a tale, known among the children who composed it as
"The Story," in which each child in the nursery took his
turn before they went to sleep in adding a chapter. To
listen to this process was to see an example of the
growth of pure and powerful narrative English which
I have not seen matched anywhere. The story itself was
enriched by suggestions by each of the four; by inquiry
as to the reasonableness of this or that adventure; by
promptings where the imagination of one or the other
was exhausted; by supplying of details if for anyone
there seemed to be a need of assistance in this direction;
by correction by the older children of the inaccuracies,
verbal or logical or practical, on the part of the younger.
And so "The Story" went on for something like five
years, constantly augmented by the growing knowledge
and experience of all the children. It ceased only when
the children grew old enough to occupy separate rooms.
I often noticed while this story was going on the method
of asking questions and the replies which were made. I
observed especially how a question induced by want of
appreciation of the viewpoint of an older child by a

younger was accompanied by an explanation that made
the matter clear, and the story did not go on until this
was done. In how many schoolrooms or homes is a subject held up, even when it is made the subject of formal
inquiry and discussion, until there is absolute clarity in
the point of view between the questioner and the questioned? And yet this is what these children demanded
naturally from each other and what they received in
response to that demand. I have rarely heard a stupid
reply to a clear question among little children. I have
often heard both stupid questions and stupid replies
among adults.

Obviously what has been said calls for a rigorous and
intelligent choice of all the material that comes to the
children of the home for the formation and nurture of
their intellectual life. There is one way and one way
only of finding out what impressions are being made
upon children by what they read and what they hear.
That way is by careful, painstaking and intelligent in-
terrogation. It may be laid down as a general principle
easily capable of verification that the subjects upon
which children develop false, dangerous and often vi-
cious ideas are those upon which there has been no free
and honest answer on the part of the parents.

5

THE ELIMINATION OF WASTE

Ease of performance and delight in achievement both grow as they are made simpler of attainment, and simplicity is generally secured by the elimination of waste. I have already spoken of the neglect to furnish materials for growth in the minds of children. But it is not enough simply to supply materials. It is also needful that waste material shall be steadily removed from the minds of children and room kept for the acquisition of fresh, new and more productive mental pabulum so that the growing child can constantly face something that challenges the maximum of his ability and does not encourage the habit of laziness, in whatever form it may disguise itself.

If you want sustained mental power, you must have the mental powers kept free from hindrances in the shape of harassing wastes that clog the mind and prevent steady and enduring concentration. The damage which comes of waste in the mind is that it prevents concentration, and there is no surer way of destroying the powers of concentration than by permitting things to linger in the mind which have no business there. This habit often causes a phenomenon with which most parents are perfectly familiar. A child, up to a certain point, seems to be developing naturally and satisfactorily; he is interested in his work and seems to be gaining knowledge and self-control and otherwise making real and substantial progress. All of a sudden he stops from no cause that can be discerned, gets careless and listless and ceases to be interested in his work. Inquiry will usually reveal that by easy stages minor and useless things have diverted the mind from its original quest. Under such circumstances there is absolutely nothing to be done but to build up the interest anew by taking out what is clogging the stream of interest, laboriously dredging out what is hindering the free and unrestrained current of mental power and attention and making possible the full use of the powers of the mind.

It is here that the necessity for clear and well-defined instruction becomes most apparent. Let an idea or a fact or a process come originally before the mind of a child crisply outlined, decisively presented and effectively illustrated and it rarely needs to be told twice! The original conception being clear, all that remains is the application of what is clearly defined in the mind.

Every ill-defined idea and every confused notion put into young people's minds is simply like dropping pebbles into cog wheels. Yet most of our textbooks are witnesses that this process has been elevated into a fine art. I have in mind at this moment my own difficulties with the so-called problems in algebra. I venture the statement—which thousands of sufferers with me will echo —that many, if not most, of the problems in algebra are not mathematical problems at all but puzzles in the English language, if such brutal stuff can be called language. I have proved again and again that once you state the equation, the student has no difficulty, and this is the important thing. But you muddle up things for the student till the main question becomes not one of mathematics but one of English, and it is supposed to be fine discipline for a young person to find out what under

Heaven the textbook maker was thinking about when he carefully hid away the elements of the question he sought to propound. One might just as well hide a needle and a spool of thread and a thimble about in a barn and set a little girl to find them and call it a lesson in sewing. For sheer stupidity and mental brutality, these so-called problems are probably unmatched in the whole theory of education. They are the rock pile of youth struggling toward mental power and self-consciousness. Students might as well be sent to mental penal servitude at once and be done with it. Nobody will ever know the anguish which has been thus heaped upon helpless young people who, under any rational dealing with exactly the same things, would have had not only interest but pleasure in performing this work. I knew an old lady who in her old age and infirmity found recreation in charades, puzzle pictures and algebra problems. The classification was both scientifically and practically sound.

The waste inherent in the vague communication of knowledge, however, is hardly to be compared with that arising from the acquisition of useless and false information through the failure to create and maintain some program for the coordination of the knowledge gained. The Bible remains incontestably the best book for general culture and most useful textbook for mental growth and maturity partly because almost everything learned from it means that about fifty other things are learned at the same time.* Knowledge of the English Bible, for

*Ed. note: Dr. Berle's enthusiasm for the Bible undoubtedly stemmed from his role as a Congregational minister. This was a book with which he was intimately acquainted. Others may wish to substitute books of similar merit with which they have great familiarity.

example, means the entrance into English literature by
the widest and most interesting gate. It means the entrance into history through the most fascinating portals.
It means the introduction to human motives by means
of the surest and most exacting standards. It means immediate, interesting and fertilizing touch with a thousand interests at once. And all these things come together at the time of life when the rudiments of
criticism are being formed and lay the foundations for
the best structural organization of the mind. Take the
most acrid portions of the Old Testament and you will
see that there is no waste in their acquisition. There is
no waste in any of this material. Hence the Bible remains the most fruitful book for the purpose of training
children.

But similar results may be secured in the intelligent
choice of other materials. There is a choice, is there not,
in giving a child a toy which excites not the slightest
effort or one that causes inquiry into what makes it go?
There is a choice, is there not, in the kind of activities
to which a child is directed? The perpetually recurring
question of young children is, "What shall I do?" That
is the opportunity of the parent, and the choice there
may be of a character which will fill with selected, intensively productive matter the inquiring young mind.
What most people do is throw anything that comes
handy to the child and get rid of thinking about it. Boys
and girls, even while not asking the question, may be
led, directed and enriched some of the time without
their knowing it. And all the time their standards of

Still, the Bible possesses considerable intrinsic merit and Dr. Berle's
reasons for using it are retained in full.

taste may be raised, their interests widened, their abilities for choice made stronger and their selective habits clarified all along the line. The degree to which this is carefully done is also the degree to which waste materials are kept out of the child's life and mind and worthwhile things substituted.

In the country village where I am writing this, there is a man who for years has done here what every parent and teacher should do. This genial lover of his kind, until infirmity prevented him from continuing his practice, used to go to the village library when it was opened for the drawing of books on Saturday afternoon and lounge around the place watching the boys and girls as they came to draw books. Friendly with them always, he used to note their perplexity and answer before it was uttered the question "What shall I get?" by a suggestion here and a bit of information there. By easy stages he got the young people to read desirable things and has for years done a most valuable work of which the young people who grew up under that practice are at this moment not even aware. One result is that more young people in this village take higher education than is probably the case in any village of its size for miles around. This man was simply preventing mental waste. Left to themselves the young people would have filled their minds simply with fiction, and probably not the best of that. As it was they got biography, travel, history, natural science and politics. That is exactly the plan which ought to be inaugurated in every household in the land. The cheap and useless stuff, tons of which are printed every year as "children's books," is not only worthless as fertilizing matter, but it is full of misinformation.

Prompt substitution of advanced material for material thoroughly digested and understood is another element in the successful elimination of waste. When do we discard one size of shoes for a child and get a larger size? When the shoes are outgrown, of course. But I have seen children wearing baby shoes on their minds long after they have outgrown them. It is a pleasant sensation to dwell upon what one knows thoroughly and thoroughly likes. Children in this respect are not unlike adults who love to read and reread their favorite authors. Now, if the author is worth reading more than once, that is one thing. But this is rarely the case with children's books, and when a child persistently is found reading the same thing over and over again, it simply indicates that the absence of mental effort involved in that process is breeding laziness and that the mind is stagnating. Something more stimulating and more exciting should be substituted promptly. Here again the Bible is an exception, because almost every text in the Bible has been commented upon so extensively that constant contact provokes increasing reflection and inquiry, which is of course the end of all mental effort. But there should be a constant and steady taking out and fresh putting in of materials which call for exertion and attention so that these faculties of exertion and attention may be kept up to their full possibilities.

The art of making everything tell toward a given result is another of the things to be noted in keeping the mind filled with fertile instead of wasteful matter. There is scarcely a subject which does not in the hands of a mature person who is interested in the work admit of endless development illustratively and otherwise. Now the more things you link with any important fact, the more you convince, first, of its importance and, second, the more surely you give it its fixed place in the mental furniture. In dealing with young people, my habit has always been to tell everything I knew about the topic under discussion. If I knew little, I made it my business to find out more. But the outstanding impression I always sought to leave was that the thing had infinite possibilities and that there was a great deal about it to be learned which was as interesting or even more interesting than that which I had already communicated. I am not above making my subject as interesting as I can and showing that there is going to be a great loss to my students if they don't take what I offer them. The lure of knowledge is the most fascinating game in the world. The child mind, eager, ready and anxious to be filled, follows any leader who has the capacity to lead. The deplorable fact is that this is a period when we give the children lies of all kinds—lies about religion, lies about social facts, lies about the family, lies about life and lies about everything that has importance and relation to sane and sound living later on. Of course, the people who do all this do not call them lies. They invent fictitious terms, but the simple fact remains that falsehoods are substituted for the truth. By and by the falsehoods are discovered to be such, and then comes the tragedy of the dropping out of the moral underpinning, the loss of confidence in those who should command it most. But the truth is not less interesting than the substitutes for it, interesting as some of these are. Certainly if the same skill were expended in telling true and great things that is now wasted in things worthless and false, the result would be astonishing.

References must be made again to the Bible because

it illustrates the point better than any other book. Your child wants a story. A very little study will embellish with sidelights and historical illustration almost any part of the Biblical narrative, and you have the best mind stuff imaginable. For older boys and girls, the interpretive word as a mature person is able to give it will acclimatize in the mind of very young people the classic authors and give them a permanent place in the intellectual affections. Anybody can prove this by simply trying it. And, by so much as this program succeeds, waste is cast out and the ground firmly and fruitfully occupied.

This process has one further and interesting result. Parents who employ it will find themselves growing skillful in anticipating possible error and in keeping misconceptions from developing, and will find themselves organizing their own knowledge in a way which without this plan they are hardly likely to do. The path of knowledge, like the path of the just, shineth more and more unto the perfect day. Soon there develops between parent and child a mutuality of understanding, an aptitude of appreciation and apprehension of meaning, and out of this arises a dialectic which is one of the best results of the entire program. Steadily there begins to recur the little tests of skill, trials of power and comparisons of judgment, by reason of the fact that the child's mind becomes aware of itself in contrast to the mature mind, and at the same time begins to take the measure of the mind which is guiding and controlling it. It may not be with some parents an uninteresting collateral result that they are taught quite as much as the child. But in any case, the worthy occupation of the mind is achieved and that of itself makes certain noxious forms of mental development impossible.

6

HARNESSING THE IMAGINATION

Imagination in children is one of the most powerful influences moving them, and to leave so powerful an instrument entirely without regulation, use and utilization is an absolutely unpardonable waste. The imaginative life of a child is usually regarded by parents and mature people merely as a pleasant source of amusement and not as a tool for the child's future development. And not a few persons to whom one mentions the idea of utilizing the imagination are repelled by the thought as in some way robbing the child of something peculiarly pleasurable and which is the child's very own and, therefore, not to be interfered with. To "harness" the imagination, therefore, will very naturally strike many persons who read this book as an unpleasant bit of utilitarianism. It springs from exactly the same feeling which persists in letting children misuse words because they are "cunning" and indulge in baby talk because it is "cute." Of course, the difficulties which are thus integrated into the child's mental fixtures to make trouble in the future are not considered. But then serious consideration for children's intellectual growth is one of the things American parents have yet to learn.

In a certain nursery with which I am very well acquainted there are upward of thirty dolls of all sizes and descriptions. Probably the whole collection with the simple exception of a large French doll, a gift to the children of this nursery, could be replaced for less than two dollars. But the value of that collection of dolls to the intellectual life and training of the children who have and still use them can hardly be overestimated. Their names will prove their peculiar relation to the intellectual interest alluded to, comprising, as they do, Cleopatra, Julius Caesar, Mark Hanna, King Edward and Queen Alexandra, Lucy and Mary (standing in this case for *Lusitania* and *Mauretania*, the great steamships), Jupiter, Cupid, John Harvard and a great many others. Here is certainly a very diversified company, and they all stand for something in particular. Now, names have figured very largely in the history of all the great human interests. Religion, for example, especially among primitive races and earlier nations, can be worked out almost entirely from the use of divine names. Names usually connote events and principles and standards of conduct or relations of one kind and another, all of which are the raw materials of thought and springs of action. Every one of the names in the above list is distinctly connected with the set of ideas which the children who own these dolls had gained and which they thought worthwhile to give permanent form. For example, the name of Cleopatra is distinctly connected with certain stories of Egypt which led directly to the investigation of other stories about Egypt and left a rather good outline of that land and its history in the minds of these children, with a variety of detail which would not be discreditable in most mature people. I recall very well when Cleopatra broke her head and, by reason of the studies to which her personality led, she was "embalmed" (another avenue of information fruitful in many directions) in a compound of olive oil, cloves, cinnamon and other ingredients which I do not now recall. While she was being buried, a Dartmouth professor happened into the home as guest and, seeing this procession going on and inquiring into the reasons for it, proceeded to give a lecture on Egyptian life and the habits and customs, as he had seen them, which has crystallized permanently a mass of additional information about Egypt in the minds of all the children. Mark Hanna was rather fully discussed one day at the dinner table in connection with an exciting political campaign in which he figured. His political generalship, his astuteness and his general representative character made a sufficient impression to cause a new little doll to be named for him. But the doll has also permanently embodied in the minds of the children the complete history of a political campaign with numerous incidents of American public life, questions of public morality which have already had and must have an increasing influence on their thought about these things as they became more experienced and mature. "John Harvard" came so early and has had so great an influence that the question of college education and preparation for it has never been discussed by these children except as to the probable date of entrance. "Lucy" and "Mary" were born out of an extensive discussion of ocean travel, of the rise, development and expansion of steamship transportation, and probably brought into the minds of the children all they were able to contain about that subject. They are the visible symbols of a distinctly understood scientific enterprise.

Now that is what I call harnessing the imagination. In this case it happened to be dolls. But it happened also with kittens who bore the names respectively of Siegfried, Tigris-Euphrates and Peter! It is a perfectly safe statement that from the doll "Helen of Troy" these children at a very early age got a full, complete and accurate account of the *Iliad* and a large section of Greek history. "Scipio Africanus" in the shape of a particularly handsome cat more than justified his existence by the increment which he brought to the children's knowledge. I have known a pet frog to embody in his title, which for obvious reasons I cannot give, the personality and outstanding characteristics of a well-known town character. Now all this was using the imagination, so to speak, for all it was worth. It gave practical things to play with, and it also stirred the mind and stored the memory with things which were intellectually fertilizing and distinctly valuable. All that it required was somebody at hand to furnish the material, and the children did the rest. The imagination was made a distinct adjunct to knowledge-getting, and with this knowledge were laid the foundations for capacity and power of comparison in a great many ways. I should like to know whether this was not quite as childlike and whether it was not infinitely more valuable than the Jessies, Fannies, and Bessies and what not, with absolutely no accompanying story? To be sure, these children had their Marys and their Lillians, who were simply creations with no history. But it remains true that the historical characters have been the abiding ones, and they are the ones which have enriched the storehouse of memory and knowledge. They also have been the ones which have furnished the greatest pleasure. This linking of the imaginative life with the sources of knowledge is one of the most fruitful fields in the intensive training of children.

As Galton says, children love to recall and recount the

stories with which the experiences that come to them
are connected. And if these stories are allied to something of intrinsic worth and interest, the gain is just so
much greater. But I know of very little use being made
of this vast power that is peculiarly strong in children.
History begun in this way will be a perennial source of
delight as long as the brain works. The field for mental
enrichment and expansion is by this tool made almost
unlimited. And it can readily be seen what an advantage is gained by a child so trained. Not only do names
connected with stories learned in childhood and stored
in the memory take away the strangeness of these
things when encountered later on, but also they are met
as old friends with whom a pleasant relationship is
resumed. They start streams of thought in many directions. They open countless conjectures about men, manners and habits of life. They make, almost without
effort, schemes of life and contrasts of appearance,
behavior and ideals of achievement which become
principles of action and almost determine the intellectual interests of later life. Children so trained are immune to the cheap and vulgar appeals to their imaginative life. From what I saw thus developed in my own
nursery I turned to others, and I have demonstrated to
my own satisfaction, at least, that almost any child will
take up almost any kind of material and assimilate it.

What I am seeking to lay down here is the principle
that the imagination needs and should receive at a very
early age direction, and that the meager equipment of
the child must be supplemented and furnished, where
the need exists, with a body and a content. All such
additions to the materials for imaginative reflection are
sheer gain. It is important to see to it that a child gets
food. But his digestion must also be watched. Exactly

the same rule applies to the mind. We must not merely see to it that the right things are brought before it. We must direct and assist in its assimilation and see that every need is supplied and that the processes of growth, and with this the formative ideas and ideals, are carefully directed—sometimes stimulated, sometimes restrained, but in every case directed.

Training and directing a child's imagination has another aspect which is of importance in his mental development. Habits of attention and concentration are, broadly speaking, the surest tests of the real strength or weakness of the mind. Attention will be held when the inward interest, called imagination, most strongly allies itself with the outward process of creating interest. The objective of creating the habit of attention is the important thing. It almost always may be secured when the imaginative elements are properly directed and controlled. And thus very early is begun the concentration of mind which is so necessary a feature of sound mentality. The right use of the imagination, instead of being a hindrance to concentration, is actually the best means of securing it. This is the case because the interest is spontaneous, because it is not projected upon the child from without, has its rise not from something outside of itself but something within craving utterance and expression. Other interests can then be allied with the original interest, and they will receive the same kind and degree of attention that the original interest received. Every time you link some bit of permanent knowledge, some fragment of literature, some incident of history, some discovery of science, with some distinct imaginative interest of the child, you have planted a seed which is sure to be fruitful in many ways.

If the harnessed imagination is an instrument of

power, the unharnessed imagination is even seven
times more destructive as a power making for mental
disintegration and discursiveness. When a man in-
dulges in daydreams and finds himself unable to fix his
mind upon the things he set to do, it simply indicates
that he has not the will power to control his imagination. But this process may be seen in its beginnings at an
early age. It is seen in commands by parents which are
unheeded, by instructions which are forgotten, by negli-
gence in a thousand different directions where the un-
controlled imagination has run away with the actuality.
The habit of lying by children often is exactly this and
nothing more. This arises from the fact that unless connected with verifiable things, linked to matters which
have distinct relation to life and actuality, with the re-
maining activities of the mind, the sense of accuracy
and veracity is impaired or destroyed.

Now the time to get acquainted with reality, even in
the realm of the imagination, is childhood. This does
not mean the destroying of dreams, but it does mean
that nobody who is truly loyal to his children will permit them to grow up with an habitually wandering
mind and playing with illusions which have no solid
foundations on the earth. The sober truth is that the
disorganization of the mind, left for any considerable
period without responsible control, tends to destroy control altogether and makes the resumption of control,
when direction is desired, a very serious matter. We live
in a world of law. The law of the mind is no less a law
when it has to do with intangible things than when it is
dealing with material matters. In children this is especially necessary because the line between actuality and
imagination is so faintly outlined in any case. Nobody

would dream of letting a little child go out into the street on a cold winter morning in its nightdress because, looking out upon the sunlit, snow-covered landscape and believing it a fairyland, the child proposed to go out without sufficient clothing. To permit this would be called insanity on the part of the parents. But it is no less irrational to permit children to take their illusions into the realities of life without guidance and without control. This also I call harnessing the imagination.

"The use of traveling," says Dr. Johnson, "is to regulate imagination by reality and instead of thinking how things may be to see them as they are." Now children cannot be great travelers. But they can be given the result of much mental journeying by the guidance and instruction of mature and trained minds. And this function, both for enriching on the one hand and for restraining on the other, belongs of right and duty to parents. It is easy to burn up the mind of a child by the extinction of the sense of reality. A harnessed imagination is likely to emerge in a chastened steady glow which illuminates without burning and which clears the pathway without blinding the eyes.

7

MENTAL SELF-ORGANIZATION

The multiplication of power through organization has become one of the commonplace observations of our industrial life. On every side we see how enterprises increase not only their efficiency but the area of their influence and utilize all sorts of collateral and allied interests in enlarging their productivity and power. So generally is the principle now understood and applied industrially that there seems to be grave danger that we shall become overorganized in some directions and sacrifice to it the power of individual initiative, which is, after all, the most valuable thing which civilization has brought to mankind.

The only domain where this enormous power of organization does not appear to be recognized is in the region of the individual life and mind. Nearly every man organizes or tries to organize his work. Comparatively few men do or try to organize themselves for greater efficiency and power. And yet the two processes are very similar, they involve almost exactly the same principles, and they bring almost the same results when the work has been properly done. It is not less possible to organize selfhood and create a compact and thoroughly effective mental organization for oneself than it is to so relate mere things as to make each supplement and help the other. The various capabilities of the mind and the various interests of the mental structure are, in fact, so far as we can judge, planned for just such coordination. And it would naturally seem to be the first business of life, and the earliest as well, to make the adjustments in a manner to secure the highest and best results.

The first business in education of any sort should contemplate just this matter. It is the ability to apply all previous knowledge to a new theme and to bring to bear all former experience and contact with facts and interests upon the fresh question propounded which gives the aspect of a disciplined mind. It is, in fact, mental organization.

Take now the simple observation here set forth and apply it to any preparatory or high school, and observe what happens. The great mass of boys and girls rarely carry the information they secure in one department to another. They rarely apply the principles learned in one sphere of inquiry to the problems of another. The information they have secured seems to be packed away like legal documents in separate boxes which are taken out and opened and examined when that particular thing is mentioned. In fact, we are seeing exactly this thing in the highly specialized education of today where an expert in one department is just a little proud of the fact that he does not know anything about anything else, holding that this in some mysterious way makes him more competent and effective in his own area.

Now the process of coordinating knowledge and establishing a mental organization is, like all other processes, easiest when the mind is most free from hindrances and while the powers of acquisition are most keen and sensitive, which, of course, means the period of very young childhood. What has been said about language and language study will apply here with conspicuous force because words and forms of words,

phrases and word stems, can be carried over from one
department of knowledge to another with telling power
for welding together the *facts* of one department with
those of another. The same words used in different relations, in differing senses and with varied applications
make one of the best means for securing the result
desired. The stimulus to find relations becomes a habit
and when the habit of finding other relations than the
obvious one, or the one directly in view, is established,
the business of mental organization has fairly begun.
And when this process is begun in a young child, it has
an advantage which no amount of mere cramming or
industrious memorizing of isolated facts can possibly
match. The reason why it so often happens that a student can get good marks in a given subject and appear
from examination papers to know a considerable
amount about a subject, and yet betray in five minutes
of conversation absolute stupidity and helplessness in
the region with which the examination seems to imply
familiar knowledge, arises from precisely what has
been just stated. Facts have been crammed into the
mind ready to be pulled out for an examiner. But there
has been no coordination of these facts with other facts
which makes them usable for anything but an examination paper. The same thing can be shown in many
other ways. It is a possible explanation why often an
honor man proves so disappointing a member of society
after leaving college.

Mental self-organization, however, is not merely the
multiplication of knowledge. It is the development of
selfhood as well. And here comes in, perhaps, the most
important element of the whole problem of child training. Such organization is really training in the use and

application of will power. The intellectual discoveries
made through the application of principles learned in
one department of knowledge to the problems and development of another almost irresistibly breed a purpose to do this kind of thing constantly and make for the
growth of the will to study, the purpose to know, the
habit of inquiry or whatever you choose to call it. And,
this established, you have again another steel girder of
the mental organization in place. The will to study, the
purpose to know, generally flags when the mind con-
ceives and originates nothing on its own account. But
give it constant exercise in originating, give it a steady
display of its own power to make fresh and original
applications of its own skill and knowledge, and you
stimulate naturally and strongly the disposition and the
habit of doing this thing.

Anyone who has had anything to do with children as
students must have observed the time come when the
child's mind seemed automatically to stop. The child
stops listening, begins to play with something or fidgets
and wants to be released. Just what has happened at
that moment? Very probably the child has become tired
of simply being stuffed with things, however excellent
in themselves, which did not relate themselves to anything which was already in the child's mind or within
the sphere of the child's interests. But if you begin with
the things which are the matters of supreme interest to
a child, you have instantaneous attention. You show
that the play, the last book read, the tennis court, the
bicycle, the wheelbarrow, the water barrel, to mention
only some of those which I myself have used, illustrate
principles of geology or geometry or geography or a
hundred other things, and every one of these things

becomes a subject of attention and scrutiny for further relations. You thus make the interest in knowledge equal to the interest in the play or diversion; in fact, you hitch the two together and very often your boy will come from the tennis court with some observation about angles about which his mind has been subconsciously working while he was having his fun. He will come back from digging in the sand with remarks about Caesar's ramparts, using his Latin terms for them, showing that subconsciously he has been applying what he learned in his last lesson. He will astound you by comparing some tiny rivulet, in its pathway in the garden, with the process of erosion, and there you are! That is what I call mental organization, and when a child begins to do that, he begins to organize himself. And what he organizes himself is his very own and constitutes his reserve stock of mental power for the grasp and attack on new things.

Now, children can be taught a thoroughly scholarly and scientific method of going about these things which they need not alter throughout life. For example, some years ago a group of children trained by this method had learned that the *Encyclopaedia Britannica* was a storehouse of all kinds of interesting information, and if you wanted to know anything about a given subject, that was a good place to seek the information. They happened to read an interesting article on the subject of chess and chess players. They had never seen chessmen nor did they know the slightest thing about the game. Interest being aroused, one of them suggested finding out more about it. They got down the *Britannica* and found the article on chess, found that it could be played on a checkerboard, which they had, devised impromptu chessmen and learned the game from that article by simply taking one statement after another and working it out. They all play chess with pleasure and considerable skill and not less so because of the rather unusual way in which this knowledge was acquired. What interested me, however, was not that they had learned to play chess but that they had learned to play a far more important and useful and, to me, more exciting game: the pursuit of knowledge. Nor was it surprising that at a later period, when it came to laying out a tennis court, they got the proper dimensions from the same source. Now the significance of all this is not that they got the facts they wanted. But they had so organized themselves and their resources and had so familiarized themselves with at least one tool of knowledge that they had made their own a scholastic method that is daily employed in every scholar's study in the land.

Of course, at first blush, it seems somewhat uncanny and unfitting to see a rather small child struggling with a big encyclopedia. But is it any more uncanny, except for habit and association, than to see a small child with a big express wagon or a big tricycle or any other object twice as big as itself? The fact is we have accustomed ourselves to imagining that the child mind must be kept in the region of the trivial, stupid and foolish and have oftentimes rigorously excluded all the serious things which not only would prove as natural as the others to the child but far more interesting. The latter have a far greater natural relation to the growing child intellect and the capacity and desire for self-expression and self-organization which every healthy child feels. There is no doubt about this whatever. All that he usually wants is opportunity and intelligent guidance. The child will usually do the rest and supply the natural suggestion for the next step in any given direction.

Concentration through the trained will is the secret of all successful self-organization. I know nothing that so develops self-government and self-regulating energy as the process I have described above—namely, that of coordinating all kinds of knowledge so that application of that which pertains to one thing or one department is smoothly and promptly applied to another. In a child it can be readily and effectively taught. It is the secret of effectiveness in study and self-subordination to a particular task. In a certain measure it is also the secret of happiness in life.

Mental self-organization brings in its train another beneficent result which is of greatest importance in study and life: the maturing judgment. It is impossible for any length of time to practice bringing the knowledge of one department into every other department of knowledge without gradually coming to compare the relative usefulness and availability of what has been gained. Thus a truth which is found to be true in half a dozen different forms of mental effort soon, by that fact, acquires a place in the mental machinery which is firmer and of greater weight than one not so generally capable of application. Children do this quite as readily as older people if they are given the chance, and while they do not call it "judgment," that is, in fact, what it is, and thus the habit of comparison and exact observation with a view to comparison steadily grows. Moreover, it develops scrutiny on first acquaintance with the ultimate end in view, and thus you have developing the habits of foresight and inference which lead to careful and sound reasoning. This is particularly true in matters of natural history and sciences and in the thousands of simple facts about life which are within the range of common experience.

Now, there remains but one more step after these have become habitual and that is to make the organization work. And the means to this is expression. When a child has done anything capably, the impulse is to express the satisfaction in the achievement, and here all the previous training combines to get an expression which is cogent, clear and precise. So finally you have secured just what all education should bring about—namely, the power to observe, to apply, to infer and to express the results of all these mental operations. After these have been established even in an elementary way you have the basis for personal self-government and personal self-examination, and whatever comes into the mental hopper will have to be ground through subjected to these processes. That is how you get a trained mind, a full mind and a balanced mind. That is how you make a mind that finds its springs of action in itself and not in others. Thus you build up self-organization steadily and surely and limited only by the amount of time and attention bestowed upon it and by the capacity and industry of the person who directs the work.

Among the hundreds of letters which I have received on this subject there is a general inquiry about the question of dealing with the will power of children when it takes the form of obstinacy. When children are "obstinate," people generally assume that the child has a "strong will." But in fact an obstinate child has usually a weak rather than a strong will and the obstinacy is the evidence thereof. Obstinacy arises from want of interest and inability to catch the threads of thought around which interest and will-subjection are trained. When not due to physical causes, it shows simply that greater effort must be made to match the natural interests and tendencies of the child with more interesting experiences and greater personal force of mentality by the parent.

Throughout this discussion the reader will not be deceived, of course, by the employment of certain terms into imagining that all these things are attained at once or in highly developed forms. That is not the important thing. The important thing is that the mind shall be started right and not be left creeping when it ought to be walking; and that it should not be kept in bondage when it ought to be developing freedom; that it should not be permitted to indulge itself on feeble stuff which makes no draft upon its growing and acquisitive powers when it ought to be kept trained day by day for severe tasks and build up strength which is resident in itself rather than dependent upon outside stimulus and outside nutrition. Mental foraging should be encouraged, books of all kinds being left for casual examination and for the momentary impulse to look at them and sometimes into them. Materials for inquiry and comparison should be furnished in variety and abundance and no inquiry left to caprice or carelessness and never to indolence. When the attention is arrested in any direction, its possibilities should be explored. When interest develops in any form, its collateral relations, especially for mental organization, should be examined and the fixed laws of mental development promptly hitched to that interest. The attention and instruction thus bestowed in the few early years of childhood will convince anyone who gives them that there is almost no subject the elements of which cannot be firmly, clearly and rationally fixed in the child mind; that it is not necessary to deal with trivial things, which pass with the using, but the serious, abiding principles of human knowledge may be implanted at a period when most people still indulge in baby talk with their little ones and hold up their hands in horror when someone proposes that it should begin to be prepared for the serious work of life.

8

TRAINING THE WILL

Most of the modern doctrines of freedom for the child strike me, in practice, as pure foolishness. I do not believe in tyranny, or in brute force, or in the kind of subjection that tortures or disfigures young life. But I am heartily opposed to the notions of child freedom, which I know can ultimate only in undisciplined helpless beings who can resist no desires, can withstand no temptations, and can concentrate on nothing long enough to be of any vital service to themselves or the world.

I have watched this matter now for a good many years. I have seen grow to manhood and womanhood a whole generation whom I knew as little children, and I have no hesitation in saying that, broadly speaking (there are exceptions of course to every rule), where they were held to regular obedience, made to recognize the rules of rightful authority, held to the things which made for character and for will training, they have done well, while the cases where the theory of "child freedom" was rampant, especially that which was afraid of "breaking" the child's will, have uniformly developed weak and negligible characters and personalities, and often something worse.

There is a perfectly natural reason why training of the will is so often neglected. It is because many, perhaps most, parents are not sure of themselves. If they are good parents they feel that they are themselves culpable at many points. That is a wholesome feeling for any parent. But because we are not perfect ourselves shall we rear young ruffians? Just because we *are* so culpable we should begin early to see to it that these things do not similarly overwhelm our children. If I know myself to have a notable defect, I should all the more strive to prevent that same defect from developing in my children! I can well appreciate why we are led to be indulgent with our children, being conscious of our own defects. But to decline, on that account, to take up the task is not only gross neglect, it is something worse.

Will training comes into play first in the matter of doing what we have no desire to do. The child finds himself face to face with the eternal contradiction between what he wants to do and likes to do and what he ought to do . . . or perhaps what somebody in authority wants him to do, usually for good and sufficient reasons. Of course, if you get a child to want to do the right things all the time, that is so much clear gain and this is the ideal way. But is it not in human nature or human experience to have always what I once heard an old New Englander call your "rathers"? That is the time when the pressure must be applied, and, as stated, it begins in the cradle. Superior force of some kind has to be applied. If there is mental development enough to get it that way, well and good. If there is not, then some other way must be found. Personally I believe compulsion of the more vigorous and physical kind is not the worst thing in this world, just as a means of education in that department of human power.

It is just here, as I believe, that most fathers fail. They pay little or no attention to their children until some matter arises where the mother has not the physical

energy to meet the situation. Then, having pursued the
policy of noninterference or indulgence, till the child
has been made to believe that this is the only or the right
policy, the father breaks loose and does with unreasoning violence more than the situation calls for, and loses
his own self-respect and the respect of the child at the
same time. Neglecting the daily pressure and supervision, failing to give the requisite application of authority in season and out of season, when mild pressure
would have sufficed, it breaks out, when it does come, in
volcanic eruptions that have neither sense nor judgment in them. Then there is wonder that only bitterness
and resentment grow up. But there should be no surprise at this.

A child thus reared is one of the wronged beings in
this world—wronged not so much in the immediate act
but in the practical denial to him of learning what he
ought to learn about respect for authority and obedience
to it, by which his own sense of self-respect and self-
discipline is developed. We learn how to govern by being governed. That is why the American people are so
lawless. They have been bred up to the ideas of a fictitious "freedom" which does not exist, never did exist
and never will exist. They get no adequate conceptions
of law. They become lawless in mind and soon afterward lawless in acts. Their only idea of will is the will
to do as they please. They learn to magnify rights and
never appreciate duties. They come to believe that there
are no qualifying facts to life.

The greatest severity a child ever encounters in this
life should be met in the home. The hardest discipline
and the most rigorous standards the child ever encounters should be those of the home. All this for the greatest

of all reasons, that here the only motive that can possibly govern is love, of the right kind. The ordinary child knows perfectly well that the parent can have no other motive in the wide world for imposing severe standards than the child's own welfare. He will therefore accept severities here when he will accept them nowhere else. Love can impose severities that mere authority cannot. Therefore, love should impose them. Love knows what will have to be met in the cold and reasoning world, which has little time to make allowances and excuses. Therefore, love should make standards and impose penalties. My own children never made the slightest complaint about the imposition of any task by their teachers, because no teacher ever dreamed of demanding of them what I demanded myself. By the same token my children never presented any problem of discipline in any school they attended. I should have regarded any such problem not as a reflection upon them but as a reflection upon myself. What business have parents to require of a school that it shall teach their children obedience, good manners and respect for authority?

The indisposition on the part of most of us to put heavy requirements upon our children arises from our failure to realize how much they are capable of doing. But notice how hard the child will work under the pressure of his own desires. That same kind of concentration should be secured in following out the desire of superiors and guides and instructors also, and may be, if the demand is steady, unyielding and never intermitted. When it is, you have concentration and will power developing naturally. The issue lies in getting the attention as fixed upon the superior or controlling will as upon its own desires. When we are dealing with little

children, the primrose path of self-indulgence is so
much easier than the hard path of unrelenting insistence. You get tired yourself and imagine the child must
feel tired too. You, having other duties, make yourself
feel that this can wait, and so stop the pressure almost
at the time when victory is won. Hence the little being,
quite ready to perceive your weariness, and anxious to
be released, aids you by making the task as difficult as
possible, and so secures the victory for himself. But this
is a defeat all around because every such victory is a
weakening of the child's own perception of the need for
successfully meeting adverse forces and soon becomes
a self-deception as to the real nature of the struggle.
Never yield. Never let the child get away from the task
you have set. Having made a limit to be reached, reach
it, even if you are both exhausted in going to that limit.
It is better to be tired out than to be defeated. I know well
enough that you will say that this is barbarity. But be of
good cheer, it yields glorious fruits!

There is another important reason why this will
power must be developed early in life. There are no
people so hard to reason with as persons who have no
self-control. Indeed, it may be said, that all reasoning
power depends ultimately upon the ability to hold oneself in restraint long enough to hear the other side. You
have probably observed in argument that the individual
with whom you are arguing often seems to be paying no
attention to what you are saying but only to be pausing
till you are through talking. This means that he is not
reasoning at all. He has not learned to restrain himself
long enough to listen carefully to another's point of
view. Now, to reason you need to be able to listen. To
reason you need to be able to hold your own opinions in

check and to mark the words and ideas of another than yourself. In fact, this is the basis of reasoning. But undisciplined people do not do this, and undisciplined children are conscious only that they are not permitted to do what they want to do. That, of course, means that no information is received and no impression is made and no education results.

Of course I don't believe in striking children needlessly, or carelessly or foolishly. But I do believe in a healthy, thorough spanking as a vastly better thing than weeping in a police court. I know of the world, and human life teaches me that nature administers the sharpest kind of corporal punishment for every violation of her laws. Why not administer the knowledge of these natural forces before the time when the realization of their awful penalties and inexorable character involves not only fearful pain but often also the ruin of life and happiness? You can teach this sort of thing to a small child as readily as you can anything else. It depends upon the purpose and character of the parent! I assume that you want to make your child an effective person. Then teach him self-control, by developing his will power, not in governing things but in governing himself. That is the seat of his power and that is also the spring of his happiness and usefulness.

Do not misunderstand me as wishing to make little trembling cravens of your children. Far from it! I wish them to be erect, self-sustaining and self-controlling. I wish them not to be deceived about the world into which they are going. I wish them not to have false or foolish notions as to their relations with other people. I want them to learn at the earliest possible moment that their usefulness is bound up with wholesome and capable self-restraint. I want their brains released from the internal warfare with self, that they may strike hard and well-directed blows at iniquity, which I know and which you know will attack them the moment they leave the parental fold. I want them well formed so that they do not have to be reformed! I want them prepared to take misfortune as a part of the program of life, without being broken by it. I want them able to stand alone, if they have to, for truth and righteousness.

It will doubtless come as a surprise to many, after what has just been written, that I urge this apparently extreme subjection in the interest of liberty and happiness. Real freedom is freedom under law. In my humble judgment nobody can appreciate liberty who has not known what it is to be under law severe and thoroughly appreciated as restrictive and firmly limiting the sphere of thought and action. Then real liberty begins, and liberty achieved under these conditions is a liberty which is glorious, because it means concentration; it means endurance; it means steady fixing of the mind and heart upon ultimate, not immediate, ends; and this forms the firm underpinning of a sound and sagacious life.

Liberty and genuine freedom thus achieved are also the only sources of real happiness. It is now a commonplace that happy children are almost always obedient children. My own opinion is that the reason why freedom in children is confounded with freedom from control is that when children are happy they require no such restraints as are commonly supposed to be necessary for discipline. It is the happiness in the children that makes the discipline needless, not the fact that there is nobody in charge. This I think is the true secret of the Montessori idea of "freedom" for children. But the reason that such children do not require "harsh" measures is not that they are unrestrained but that they are happy!

To confer happiness upon a child in the interest of his will development is not the business of the child; it is the business of the parents and the home. The home authorities must bring their maturity to bear upon this problem and solve it in the light of their knowledge, not the ignorance of the child. They must develop happiness through their superior insight, not through acquiescence to the casual desires of the child. Happiness sought for the child in the interest of developing real strength of will power, not capricious insistence upon his own desire, is a capital interest for every person who has anything to do with children.

9

THE ADOLESCENT STORM

That children arriving at the age of puberty find themselves in an epoch of revolt and revolution, facing new and strange things, confounded, perplexed and usually forsaken and helpless, seems to be not a question for discussion. It is one of the common facts of human life. Nobody to my knowledge has raised the question as to whether this storm period of young life is necessary or not. It seems to be taken for granted by the orthodox psychology that it must come with greater or less severity, but come it must.

But as we become enlightened we do not think things are as inevitable as we once did. We do not take the medicines we used to take. We drink water now in fevers when we used to be almost roasted alive by the denial to us of drink. And so of a great many other things. I absolutely refuse to accept as final the doctrine that there must necessarily come to every emerging man or woman a period of anarchy. The transition from boyhood to manhood will always come. But there will also come a time when that transition will not be accompanied by irresponsibility and unreason. There will always be a time when the girl ceases to be a girl and becomes a woman, but it will not always be a time when she has to become a lawless, wild, unreasoning or terrified creature instead of a human being. I do not know how this will be achieved, but I believe it will come, and I am about to make some suggestions which in my judgment will have some bearing on the discussion.

It is hardly to be wondered at that when children arrive at the adolescent stage, if they have nothing in their heads, they are the natural prey to the passions that are roused in them, especially if they have had nothing that throws the slightest light on what they are experiencing, and have known nothing in the way of strong government or in will control. But is it or is it not reasonable to suppose that, if you begin to give a child very early in life material worthy of thought and to fill the mind with interesting things that have to do with himself, the world in which he lives, the people and surroundings in which he moves, the world of nature, science and literature, you have built a powerful fortification against the attacks of adolescence, and possibly neutralized them entirely?

Take the average child of about twelve, reared carelessly, never having been compelled to use his mind intensively, never having had to learn by any severe government any effective self-control, and imagine there suddenly breaking into the life of such a child the eruptive influence of manhood or womanhood! Is there anything strange in the fact that such a being should be bowled over and should easily fall prey to the worst influences that come to it, especially if no relationships of confidence on this and allied subjects have ever been established between the child and his parents?

With a full mind the child will have the materials for self-control within himself and will not be thrown overboard the first time something strange or unusual happens. If his powers of observation have been developed at all, he will at least hold still long enough to think some things through and perhaps get good advice from somebody. If the moral relation between the child and the parent had developed naturally, through the intellectual method of companionship, conversation and study of things together, it is my judgment that the over-throw will not come in the vast majority of cases. We all have volcanic eruptions, of course, and life itself brings many occasions and temptations. But what is rational and sound development but the steady reduction of the number of things which are beyond our control?

I am not presumptuous enough to believe that this subject can be disposed of in a single chapter like this. I am fully aware of all the facts in support of the ortho-dox theory of adolescence. However, I also believe that the increase in mental life and power, the development of intellectual interests, will materially tend to rob this period in the life of the child of its terrors.

This if it is understood also does not to me imply the slightest loss of physical power to any child so trained. I would not take from any child one whit of his full physical power and capacity. I believe in it. I believe it necessary to will power. I believe it needful to mental force. I believe it necessary to sound human relations and durable happiness in life. But by these very tokens, I believe in educating the child to the point where, when this new element comes to life, he will have the re-sources to meet it.

10

BREEDING INTELLECTUAL AMBITION

Intellectual ambition has the first opportunity with the child, and the loss of it is, therefore, even more reprehensible in those who suffer it to be lost. A young child cannot take a very large part in affairs until his physical abilities are very considerably developed. He has his games and play, to be sure, but these are within a very limited area. His mental life, on the other hand, may be worldwide almost from the start through the processes which I have already described. His intellectual interests may be diversified, entertaining, alluring and exciting in a thousand directions before the little feet are able to kick a football or he has the command over his arms required to catch a thrown ball or over his legs to run a base successfully. The mind works a thousand times as fast as the physical structure. You can see this any time by asking a child to write what he has told you so brightly and interestingly in an oral discussion. You will see at once that his hands are undeveloped and the muscles of his arms stiff and unpliable, and hindrances at every turn fret and prevent him from moving in quick response to his mental activity. That is simply because the mind moves much more rapidly than the body possibly can. Thus it comes about that ambitions of an intellectual kind, which have their origin in vivid mental images, picturing the vast influence of mind, or in powers which are the evidence of great mental force, or social and spiritual revolutions which are the immediate outworking of the powerful thought, really have the right of way in the child mind. The only reason why that primacy is not maintained is because it is neglected. By regular stages the physical life is permitted to become the ideal life. The book gives way to the sword or the gun or the football or something else. The games follow largely along similar lines, and by the time the boy or the girl comes to the place where the blossoming mind should begin to realize some of the things that it has been contemplating with longing, he has become deflected from the intellectual to the physical ideal, if he happens to be a boy, or the social ideal, if she happens to be a girl, and the ambition to excel intellectually remains only as a desirable asset which may possibly be secured, but only through a process which is necessarily long and very unpleasant. In this, of course, the false use made of some of the noblest emotions materially aid. Patriotism means to fight for your country. Hence the idealization of the soldier, the sailor, the battleship and the man behind the gun. The triumphs of science, of art, of culture, of statesmanship are neglected, partly from want of appreciation and partly from incapacity to present them, and the ambitions of the child sink into lower and more material channels.

While all this is going on, there is probably no passion of the American people about which they feel themselves so sincere as the passion for education. But if it is really as sincere as it seems to be, and there are grave doubts on this point, it is woefully misdirected and helpless. I do not believe a man when he tells me that he wants above all things a thorough education for his child and then does not make the slightest effort from one year to the next to acquaint himself with the means and the persons and the institutions, public and private, which are giving or failing to give his child the education so highly extolled. Yet this is what we see on all sides. The wrongs done to young children by the neglect of their intellectual ambitions and aims by their parents is one of the wickedest things about the American home. It is losing to the American people taste, culture, civilization and social advances of incalculable worth. But above and beyond this, it is losing for a large fraction of the human race happiness and delight beyond computation.

American parents for the most part do not want advice. They want what they call "results." But the sagacious woman who had a perfect educational plan, Dr. Maria Montessori, an expert scientist, a physician, and a dietician to boot, knew that all these things could be nullified by an attitude, and so the longest single paragraph in her entire code of regulations applies not to the duties of the children, and says absolutely nothing about what she intends to do with the children when she has them, but deals entirely with parental obligation. There could be no more striking evidence of the place which the home or its equivalent holds in the gifted educator's mind than the regulations which she framed and which were intended to provide her with what she needed first and foremost—freedom to do her work in her own way, not only without parental interference but also with obligatory parental cooperation. Even this gifted educator and scientist will not match herself against a hostile or an indifferent home.

Human beings insensibly grow to be like what they are taught to admire, and if the admirable qualities of the intellectual life are made clear to the young child, he will love knowledge as much as he loves anything else. It is but simple truth to say that we have not expected little children to take any interest in the great heroes of the intellectual life and consequently they have been given over to the heroes of lesser accomplishments. I can well recall as a child visiting the home of one of my playmates and being introduced to a gentleman who seemed to be doing all the talking while the family listened with reverence and rapt attention to what he was saying, and, asking afterward who he was, I was told, "He is a scholar!" with an air of finality that assumed that I ought to know that a "scholar" was a person of such distinction that everybody ought to keep silent and listen. It is not strange that every one of that family of boys, five in number, who that evening listened to their visitor, impressed with the reverence which was felt by their parents for a scholar, themselves became scholars and form a remarkable group of men in the community where they live. Though engaged in widely differing pursuits, they are scholars all of them.

When we speak of an ambitious child, we usually mean a child who has found a specific direction in which he wishes to go. And that will ordinarily be found to be a child who by some process, natural or unnatural, has had his attention kept fixed on something that he has been led to admire. Why should the admirations of a child be left to accident or caprice? Why should we not select the things which we wish the youth to love and point out with exactness and care what is desirable, what is beautiful, and the good report in connection with them? And why should not such a process be the result of a distinct plan and kept distinctly outlined as a part of the child's development? I have interviewed many successful men in many callings of life and have uniformly found that they were inspired to make the efforts which made them successful men by some personality, sometimes a living model, sometimes a historical character, who had so arrested their attention that they felt an irresistible desire to follow in his footsteps. All of which suggests a phase of this subject which should cause deep reflection on the part of parents. The love of parents, strong in most households up to a certain point, makes the father and mother the working models of manhood and womanhood. In this matter example is much more powerful than precept.

Why do certain families send representative after representative to the great football teams of the great colleges? Because the one subject which the younger boys hear from their elders is football, and they plan to be football stars as much as they plan to be men. And, given the requisite physical equipment, they usually are. If you do the same thing with scholarship, you will get scholars.

Emerson says, "Each man is a hero and an oracle to somebody; and to that person whatever he says has an enhanced value." This truth, true of all persons, is trebly true of children in the home. If the father chooses to be a hero to his sons, he may be one and remain one to the end of his days. If the mother chooses to be a heroine to her daughters, she has the first and the best chance with her own children. If father and mother let that distinction go to somebody else, it is their own deliberate choice. That should be understood by every parent in the land. And if it is thoroughly understood, it will be seen that not only is great power transferred by

this enormous influence but likewise enormous responsibility shirked. It must be true from what we see before
us everywhere that parents either do not think about
this matter or deliberately abdicate from the throne of
influence with their children. We often speak of what is
bred in the bone. But what is bred in the bone is comparatively unimportant beside what is bred in the
thought, experience and idealizing tendencies of children at an early age.

Breeding intellectual ambition has another important function which must be noted in dealing with this
subject. The moment you have roused ambition in a
child you have created a fresh source of power within
the child's mind and at the same time placed there a
sense of responsibility, insofar as it relates to effort, instead of a dependence on authority exercised from without. Once ambition is aroused the process of auto-educa-
tion begins—self-examination, self-discipline and self-
direction—crudely enough at first, but nevertheless
clearly apprehended and acknowledged. This leads to
independent efforts which are more valuable in their
mental result than all formal education. Spencer refers
to this in his essay on education when he says:

Any piece of knowledge which the pupil has himself acquired,
and any problem which he has himself solved, becomes by
virtue of the conquest much more thoroughly his than it could
else be. The preliminary activity of mind which his success
implies, the concentration of thought necessary to it and the
excitement consequent on his triumph conspire to register all
the facts in his memory in a way that no mere information
heard from a teacher or read in a school book can be regis-
tered.

It is clear enough here that the important thing is to
inspire that effort, to cause the child to want to do some-

thing worthwhile so much that he will get the "mental tension" and the "activity of mind" incidental to the satisfaction which he craves. Notice, too, that failure in this direction and under these conditions is not failure at all. The increment gained from a solid effort precludes serious distress, because the exercise of the faculties has so greatly increased the consciousness of power.

The habit of aiming at a great result, of looking to an ultimate instead of an immediate goal or effort, tends to enlarge the mental powers and expand the mental horizon in children as it does in adults. Once you get young persons in the way of looking for something that is palpably great and as palpably beyond their easy reach, you get the same kind of action in the mind that you see in the arms of a small child reaching for an object upon a shelf just beyond his reach. The objective point may not be reached, but the effort has strengthened the mental fiber; it has felt its possibilities, it has tried itself for an end; demanding the best that is in it, and this habitually done, will breed personal determination and perseverance which are simply ambition at work. It is not material just how the effort works out. But as a matter of fact, nine times out of ten the child succeeds and immediately tries for something still higher. But to inspire this effort the memory must be stored with high thoughts and splendid deeds which call for intellectual activity, and the vision must be kept fixed upon the great personalities who have enriched the thought of the world.

11

THE PLEASURES OF THE MIND

Perhaps the general impression upon many readers of what has been previously written will be a feeling that, as desirable and profitable for the child's future and his advancement in life and usefulness as all these things may be, the price that it demands is too great to be paid. Many parents assume that worthwhile activities of the child mind are necessarily devoid of pleasure and that somehow the consideration in childhood of what afterward constitute the serious studies of life despoils children of pleasure, vitiates the natural freedom and artlessness of children and prematurely induces solemnity of mind and sedateness of behavior. Let me assure every person who holds this view that there is possible no more mistaken assumption than this. I have at this moment come in from the meadow adjoining my summer home where I have officiated as "catcher" in a "battery" where a very young person, just past his tenth year, officiated as "pitcher." For an hour I sweated, ran, dodged and jumped around trying to perform the duties of this onerous position to the satisfaction of the young twirler who is planning to make a baseball record along with the rest of his ambitions. Previous to the baseball episode he had been put through an hour lesson in verbal analysis, and immediately succeeding the play another lesson in Latin was taken up. It can be said with absolute truthfulness that the delight in the first and third periods was not only not less but if anything more than that in the baseball achievements.

Mental activity and mental effort as sources of pleasure have rarely been adequately considered by teachers generally, and the pleasure motive to study is almost
absolutely ignored by both parents and teachers. Many
teachers do at times observe the pleasure of children
when they have done any work satisfactorily but, for
some reason or other, probably the assumption to which
I have referred, avoid making use of the pleasure motive in inducing special advance in this direction. But I
cannot see why a child should not be taught and guided
to seek pleasure in one kind of exercise as well as in
another. Here again the child generally knows how to
play one thing and does not know how to play the other.
It is a question often of which game it knows best, and
if the games of the mind were as steadily taught and as
carefully outlined in one instance as in the other, you
would get substantially the same results. How many
times a little girl making the first doll clothes comes to
the mother or nurse for instruction! And it is usually
given because here various kinds of motives combine in
the parent's mind to give the needed lesson, often with
extraordinary care. The same thing is true of the boys
who want to be taught things that relate to the athletic
field. But how many people ever give the child an exhi-
bition of the pleasures which they themselves have in
some distinctive mental achievement! How often is a
fine paragraph in a book or a specially beautiful passage in a classic poem read and its excellences shown to
the child, its imagery praised, its force and power extolled and the desire for emulation aroused? The assumption that this has no interest for the child is wholly
gratuitous.

Get it once into the youthful mind that mental effort
and mental achievement are the great glory of human

beings and bring into the foreground of its consciousness not the gladiators of history but its statesmen, its
thinkers, its scientists, its philanthropists, and you have
furnished, first of all, a means of comparing results
which almost any child will comprehend very quickly.
History is full of examples, and the instinct of hero worship tends to reinforce the example. But if all your
heroes are warriors, your child will want to play with
drums, guns and swords. If the major part of his notion
of great men and great works is connected with destruction, experiments in this art at a very early stage will be
provoked. But if your heroes are the heroes of science or
the heroes of humanity, you create mind stuff that re-
bels without effort against destruction and starts out
with entirely opposite notions of activity and self-
expenditure.

The pleasure that the child experiences and of which
it gives the most instant signs is more than exceeded by
that of the parent or teacher who thinks along this line.
I know nothing so fine and so thoroughly satisfying as
to see the mind of any human being working soundly
and smoothly and with apparent self-regulative power.
And to see this process in its early stages, growing in the
child's mind, is a very delightful sensation. You get the
happy consciousness that your own mental processes
are sound because your errors will be repeatedly thrown
back at you in large letters like the big hand of a child's
penmanship. You will have a constant corrective for
yourself and you will unconsciously be kept on edge, so
to speak, to make your own power more accurate, your
own insight more acute and your habits more careful.
And instead of being irksome, the first time you see your
own effort eventuating in a fine effort on the part of the

child, only improved with the child's simplicity, natu-
ralness and artlessness, taking on naturally what you
have laboriously acquired by heavy self-subordination
and self-restraint, you will feel that you have made a
genuine contribution to the fullness of the life of mankind. In fact, you have made such a contribution because his generation will do almost by nature what you
have had to acquire by effort, and a real and permanent
advance in the standard of humanity has been made.
And as one capacity after another develops and they
begin to cooperate and you see growing up about you
healthy, sane, self-controlling and self-directing individuals who are as mentally strong as they are mor-
ally sound, you will feel that the hero who has simply
killed so many thousands of people is a mere slaugh-
terer and not worthy to be mentioned by the side of one
father or mother who advances by ever so small a degree the type of humanity by which this world is to be
inhabited. It looks like extracting a very great and por-
tentously big satisfaction from one insignificant little
baby! But it is there for every parent who will take the
trouble to find it.

The pleasures of the mind last longer than any others.
Bodily pleasure at best has its necessary limits. The
shouting and the tumult of physical satisfaction even of
the best sort die and disappear. But the genuine pleasures of the mind last forever. They have a staying quality which enriches advancing years and forms the natural linkage with the growth of the world. Everyone must
have noticed the differences between the kind of people
who at any age seem to be in touch with what is going
on and who read with delight and avidity the newest
things that are taking place everywhere in the world

and others not so constituted. I have in mind such a man, an octogenarian now, who is the youngest person I know. His childhood was such a childhood as I have described in the foregoing pages, nurtured, fertilized, trained and enriched at every turn, and his old age finds him one of the most active men of the community, keen in intellect, stored in learning and a perennial source of pleasure to all his friends by the sumptuousness of his remembrance of personal and historical lore. Mental pleasures last.

When shall these mental springs be opened? After ten or a dozen valuable years have been lost, when the edges have already been dulled, when coarse and ugly things have already integrated themselves into the juvenile intellect and, weedwise, sought the best places and fixed their tenacious grip on most fertile spots? Shall we wait till mature life has shown the seeds of self-distrust and doubt, made suspicion a habit and organized the antagonisms of the mind behind which lurk enemies, real and imaginary, to be overcome at every turn? Or, when the unclouded intelligence first looks out on the world, surrounded only by affection and unconscious of the great issues to be fought, and steadily strengthened by supervision, by instruction, by the ever-widening circle of information, by self-equipment through organization of the mind, till, when it breaks forth into the world, its strength is as the strength of ten not only because its heart but its mind is also pure? Most people give only one answer to these questions. Open the mind of youth to the best, they say, promptly and with no hesitation at all. But who shall do it? Who will take from the moments of self-indulgence a few, to give them to the work of thus enriching the child by his side? Who will make the child the first and most supreme interest, and make social enjoyment, travel, amusements and all that these imply secondary? That is the great question. No school can do what the school in the home can do and ought to do. No educational establishment can possibly achieve that first and greatest success for education, which is won in the home, where the first things are kept first and where lofty and beautiful ideals crystallized in the memorials of knowledge through the works of the great intellectual leaders are among the earliest associations of the child mind.

Why should my little nine-year-old be told all about the struggle concerning the House of Lords, its entire history carefully rolled out before him, its great names identified, its place in English history illustrated and recounted in forty different forms and methods to give him a vivid picture of what the present political revolution in England really means? Is that matter for a child? Why not let him have the exhilaration of simply wasting his emotions on the momentous question of whether the Tigers or the Athletics will win? Simply because I choose the remoter pleasure, leaving aside for the moment all else, that when he is twenty-five or possibly less and, in the revolutionary progress of history, the House of Lords will be in English life what a horsecar is in the streets of a modern city, if it is there at all, he will have among the permanent furnishings of his mind the events which have made history and life for him what it then will be and have them stored up for the many varied uses. That information which others laboriously seek out in books and libraries will be habited in his mind. But above and beyond all these, he will have the pleasure of recalling that this history is also allied to his

home, to his child life, to the dearest and best associations which this world brings and will, when that subject is mentioned (as will be true of many hundreds and
perhaps thousands of other themes), give him the pleasure of seeing in his mind's eye his childhood home and
the faces of those whom he has loved long since and lost
awhile. Is there anything more alluring than this? Is
there a more beautiful and worthwhile task to exalt the
parental mind or charge the parental heart with zeal
and patience?

Thus there is established a reciprocal intellectual relation that is pleasurable beyond anything else in life.
In extent, there is nothing whatsoever that matches it.
It not only fills this life but it reaches far beyond. Many
people whose intellectual traditions reach beyond a single generation can readily recall things that came to
them from the elder day by inheritance, so to speak,
which merely means that they have been inculcated
naturally and formed the mind stuff of daily existence
and thought. When new letters or memorials of such
elders are unearthed and when the treasures of memory
are unlocked and one sees the power of the continuous
stream of knowledge-loving people, not necessarily
professionally engaged in the so-called intellectual callings, there is the peculiar pleasure of being in the
stream of that life and the natural representative of
certain things that have come down from other days.
Sometimes the profession is handed down from father
to son for generations in this way. Sometimes certain
responsibilities, civic, philanthropic and otherwise, are
handed along from one generation to another, and the
public expectation demands, as the natural responsibility creates, definite attitudes and services to the community.

It seems to be reasonably well settled that the struggle for existence will steadily grow harder and also that in the future, though the competitions in some directions will undoubtedly be lessened, in others they will be highly intensified. Once in the struggle, there is little hope that men will take time for this kind of culture and the kind of life which such culture requires. The ideas and the ideals must be firmly planted in the heart and thought of early youth. One does not have to be a seer, sitting in a streetcar and looking into the worried faces of men and women, to know that most of these people have no real peace of mind and not many resources which make for serenity within or joy in the work of life. It is easy to see that in many of these people imagination has utterly perished. It is easy to see that the capacity for real and even recreational pleasure in many cases has disappeared.

The joy of life springs from the sources of joy and is not pumped into life by buying admission to a place labeled amusement, just as education is not to be secured necessarily at a place called college. Joy comes from real alignment with the things that make for security, contentment and peace. Deep down at the sources of life, before birth in many cases, but at birth and immediately thereafter, certainly are the foundations of life to be laid. And the spirit in which they are laid must be that which contemplates a result so sublime that all the imaginative powers are stirred to their utmost to make them secure and strong and capable of upholding the greatest superstructure that can possibly be laid upon them. Who can know but that this small creature whom you can hold almost in the palm of your hand will one day be the pivot upon which some vast and mighty human interest will revolve? It is no impertinence for any mother to think this possible. The importance and supremacy of the individual will never be reduced however society develops. To take a large and comprehensive view of the possibilities of life for the humblest child is not only not presumption but is the only true view, at least for the parents who brought him into the world. In the home school will his earliest and most effective lessons be taught. In the home school will his first and substantial ethical outlook upon life be developed. In the home school will the permanent joys of life and the springs of life be uncovered. But these springs are within, and they are found only by the patient, persistent and intensive utilization of the earliest moments of life.

BERLE'S SELF CULTURE

12

INTRODUCTION

Self culture is a compendium of knowledge and an arrangement of literature, science and the arts by which any household that makes a careful and faithful study of it may obtain the elements of a liberal cultivation.

One of the most important of the many values of such a collection as this is that it tends to preserve the mental relationships of the entire household. Age differences tend to separate homes by making the interests of the various members so diverse and so isolated from those of the other members that there is frequently little mental communion between them. This we have sought to avoid, because in that home unity of mental life lies the best fruitage of each. Adults should not be wholly apart from children in their intellectual materials of thought and feeling. Children should gain from their elders their original impressions as to what is good and beautiful in literature and knowledge.

Take down a volume every day and read something aloud to the whole household, and make it a subject of discussion afterward.* That will be the best possible use made of this work. An excellent plan in this direction, and the one that I have followed in my own family for

*As noted in the first chapter, the various volumes which compose *Self Culture* are available in other, more easily obtainable forms, at minimal expense. These materials are reviewed in more detail in the last chapter under the section entitled "The Inquiry Method."

many years, is to bring to the evening meal a volume and read a few pages from something interesting, the choice being made on inclination or suggested by something heard or written during the day, so that all the members of the household get the information and are made to think together at the same time about the same thing. It will be found that thus the children often fertilize the minds of their parents and parents give the children the benefit of their maturity. Even the smallest child who can read should take part in this plan. Nothing more delightful can be imagined than to have a small child take one of those volumes that seem like "big books" to him and read to the family one of the delightful child stories that are gathered here or some of the Bible passages that are printed here in narrative and unconventional form. Many thousands of people who have read my books and corresponded with me on the subject of child training have testified to the remarkable change in the household life which this habit has produced.

13

HOW TO CREATE INTEREST

You are now to take up a systematic course of training with your child. Let me at the outset of this course suggest to you one or two important facts that have come to me out of thirty years' experience. The first is that you do not need to be a highly educated person with a host of college degrees to do this work and do it well. What you need is that you shall have a constant desire to see this thing accomplished and take it up steadily, a little at a time, but persistently. Your own maturity, the mere experience of years, will give you sufficient lead to keep far in advance of the child, and you will be learning all the time.

The second fact I wish to impress upon you is this: let the child join you in the search for what you do not know at first hand. The best kind of teaching is learning with a child. When you are looking up something, just let the child look with you if that is possible, and when it is not possible, show the child just how you went about finding it.

The third fact is just this: jot down every day or every few days the things you have been doing, and so keep a kind of record. That will be useful to you, both as showing your own progress and the child's progress, and it will furnish you with the matter out of which your discussion of these facts and interests will grow.

You must keep in mind that the thing you must excite in the child first of all is curiosity. Every question is a sign of interest. Many times I have taken a child who wanted to know about balloons, let us say, and so guided him that at the end of the talk he wanted to know about onions or beets. Sometimes he started with shoestrings and wound up with roses. I always used to test myself by proving to myself that I could guide him around to the things that I wanted him to know rather than the first thing at hand which provoked the original question.

You must be the guide of the thought and you must plant the seed-thought. This matter of seed-thoughts is a very great fascination when once you get the habit of planting them. Take an article from any volume which is suited to the capacity of the child—a poem, a story, a descriptive article or something about science. Read it to him and with him. Occasionally stop and dwell on some of the words. Sometimes reread a sentence that has a specially interesting fact or that has a specially interesting sound. You will find many such. Pause and note the unusual words. Discuss some of them. Raise some question about them or about the fact contained, their resemblance or their dissimilarity or their rela-tion to anything of which the child has had previous knowledge or of which he has previously heard. Note what response you get. If none, try again. Get out of your own life an experience that tallies with it or that contra-dicts it. No matter what the connection is, tell some-thing out of your own life that has something to do with it. Then your own story will be called for at once.

In this manner you gradually induce the habit of not merely absorbing the things you offer but also talking them over. Just remember that there was a time in the history of the world when all knowledge in the world had to be transmitted in this way. There were no books, and each generation had to be taught all that the previous generation knew by the oral method. You will, of course, supplement and prepare the way for all this by surrounding your child with the things which call for explanation. If you place books in the room, sooner or later the books will call for attention, handling and explanation. The same is true of pictures. The same is true of simple art objects. Taste is developed in this manner much more than by formal instruction. Choice of color and the arrangement of even the simplest room has a great deal to do with these matters.

An excellent device for this sort of thing is to place the objects in a room in different positions and ask why one is preferred to another. It always seemed to me a rather important thing to have the objects a child saw on first awakening in the morning of rather special interest. I often changed pictures on the wall or placed a pretty vase or other decoration, in the summertime a bunch of flowers, where the awakening child saw it when the eyes first opened and got a little thrill of surprise or pleasure when he looked around. You would be pleased yourself to awake tomorrow and find a lovely bunch of roses by your bedside. It takes only a little care and not much time to think of these things.

See that you stimulate your own interest while stimulating that of your child. For many years whatever interested me for my own sake made a good rule for interesting my children in the same thing. For example, I am interested in painting and sculpture. Very well; I used to note the new paintings and new works of sculptors. Being interested myself, I showed them to my children, and they naturally grew up with that as a permanent interest in their lives. The same thing was true about poetry. Their mother loved plants and knew a great deal about botany, and hence they got the same kind of interest in flowers and gardening.

This is equally true when it comes to the story of human life and action. Geographical matters, or stories of discovery, or adventure, or dramatization of life events through biography, open the gates here very wide indeed. Every week in the year should introduce the name of a great figure to the household. If you stick up on the wall, week by week, one such name—you can easily print it yourself, with a few facts about him or her—you will be surprised what will happen, because when you compare one great man with another you will have started the science of conduct and the profoundest speculations of which the human mind is capable. There is nothing so interesting as the study of human beings. And if they have had a great history and made a great mark on the history of the world, they become especially interesting.

Sometimes you can vary this biographical interest in the world's great figures by choosing some of the stories of the world's famous children. Children love to hear about other children, and this varies the interest, though, of course, child life in one sphere is often incomprehensible to children in another. The ordinary life of the children of various nations told in song and story and pictures helps here and makes a pleasant diversion.

There ought to be a rotation of interest. There should be a Father's Hour when the father should choose something, read it and explain it. Then the mother can start the questions and the rest can take part, guided by the start which the mother has given. Then there should be the Mother's Hour, when the mother should take the lead and the questioning be reversed. Then the various children should have their individual needs met, taking turns and all making themselves for the time being six-year-olds, ten-year-olds, or whatever the age is. This will develop into a very exciting sport if it is cultivated with only a little care.

Just let yourself go in this matter. Get yourself filled with some topic and then let go and give it to the best of your ability to the children. Never mind at the start how well or how ill it seems to be done. The main thing is to get the genuine interest. For this reason it will be well to attack something that is fresh to you, and you and your children can go at it together.

You must remember always that not all people, either old or young, think with the same speed. Hence you must keep a fair pace for all concerned. Don't get impatient because what is so clear to you is not comprehended at once by the rest, especially the children. I have seen parents storm at their children and call them stupid when they were simply matching the speed of their maturity against the slowness of the child's youth. Of course, that was obviously unfair; perhaps it was merely the parent's ambition which did it. But we must not forget that it is very easy to think that all others are like ourselves when they are not. So give the little people time to think; make suggestions, give little hints, help their thinking and generally pave the way, so that the little mind begins to work under its own steam.

Keep in mind another thing: merely to ask questions that cannot be answered does not mean that the person who cannot answer them is stupid. I do not at this moment know how high the Karakoram Mountains are.

But I don't care how high they are; it is not of enough
importance that I should know. It is enough that I know
where I can find out if I need to know. Keep in mind the
difference between stupid questions and useless knowledge, and usable and living knowledge. So when you
make your selection of things to read and things to talk
about, choose live matter and something that has vital-
ity.

14

THE DEVELOPMENT OF THE PLAY INSTINCT

Play is the occupation of childhood and begins in the very earliest elements of the baby's consciousness of himself and his powers. The desires to move, to pull, to stretch, to roll and to grasp are efforts at physical self-expression that eventuate in play in a little child. Child societies are play societies and the child life is play life. All the experiences of childhood are in the form of play, and every play is a new experience. This in turn gives new desires, new abilities, new feelings and new knowledge.

Properly directed, such play is the highest form of intensive education because it organizes the child's powers, leads him to make new efforts on his own account, and makes him aware of powers of which he was not aware before. This is real education. Of course, all this does not mean absolute noninterference, because the mother is the natural first playmate of her child and she should know how to be the child's playmate in order to do it effectively. This, also, because then she can guide the play, avoiding what is injurious and stimulating what is helpful and good; but guidance is not suppression of the child's initiative.

15

ENVIRONMENT AS A FACTOR IN MENTAL DEVELOPMENT

If you could look into the human skull, you would see that it is divided into two hemispheres, a right and a left lobe. All development is determined by the development of one of these hemispheres, while the other lies, as it were, dormant, ready for emergencies if anything happens to any portion of the other. Right-handed people develop the left lobe; left-handed people develop the right lobe; and this extends through the entire development of all the senses. There is a visual area, there is an aural, and so on. Now this development, as it goes on, develops tiny fibers with each repetition so that the various areas connect with each other and help each other. Therefore, all mental development is in a sense a multiple development, eye, ear and lips cooperating to fix the place in the brain and make for cooperation in the normal child.

Most people understand by environment merely physical surroundings. To a great extent this is true. Scientists have found, in examining the lives and surroundings of men of genius, that certain factors were always present—namely, abundant food, opportunities for culture, books and contact with sources of culture. It was found that most of them lived either in cities, where these things abounded, or in homes where they were possible without the city atmosphere. A home without books rarely develops high literary taste. A home without art rarely develops fine artistic taste. A child brought up in a doctor's home will usually have a deeper interest for physiology than one brought up in the home of an architect, while the latter is much more likely to know something about beauty in structure of buildings. This is merely because the child absorbs the interests by which he is surrounded, takes on the language which deals with him and describes him, and so develops a culture and attitude along these lines, because language is the instrument of knowledge. In a similar way a Greek child speaks Greek, a German or French child speaks German or French. A child reflects not merely the brick, mortar and stone of the house that shelters him, but much more the ideas which govern that house. Hence the latter are much more important. It is of higher importance to a child to live with a house full of books in the space of three rooms than in the bookless house that has twenty rooms. Mere space and physical surroundings, apart from ideas, do not make for culture, important as space is for comforting growth.

So when you think of the environment, think not only of the material, but much more of the mental environment. What does a child hear talked about? That becomes the raw material of his thinking. What does he hear praised? That becomes the basis of his taste. What does he hear condemned? That becomes the basis of his judgment. Attitudes of mind on the part of parents form the starting point for the child. Parents sometimes fail to understand that their mere attitude toward things settles some things forever for children. One must keep in mind that these little minds are capable of absorbing about fifty times as much as they are capable of expressing. You cannot tell what they are absorbing except by what you are giving them to absorb. By the time they begin to express themselves, you wonder where the child learned that, always forgetting that long before he could express himself he was absorbing what was placed before him in your life and activities.

If we want to build up a mentality that will exhibit the qualities we admire, we must exhibit those qualities themselves or permit to the child associations which exhibit them. It is an old saying that you cannot gather figs from thistles. Many wise parents live their lives over in their children and grow over with them, because thus what was denied to them in their own youth they acquired through the youth of their children. It is the best kind of mature study and growth.

16

READING TO AND WITH CHILDREN

There is no greater aid to the love of good literature than familiarity with the best that has been written in the course of the world's development, and unlike many of the good things of life, there is nothing so well within the reach of even the humblest men and women. To the average parent, therefore, the difficulty lies not so much in finding the material he needs for the task of helping his children into the larger appreciation as in selecting that which is most useful for his purpose. The purpose itself is a simple one: by home training to develop in the child an acquaintance with and liking for the best in literature. And as the instrument of this, nothing is of more importance than reading to the children and helping them to read by themselves. For it is by reading aloud to the child so young that he cannot hold the book for himself that a sense of literature is maintained.

It is on such slender foundations that the love of literature may be built. A child first learns to love the sound of words. The most elementary form of this is shown in the child who, because he likes the sound of some word or phrase, will repeat it constantly with relish and gusto, though without real understanding of its meaning. I remember a group of children who used to listen with the closest attention for the recurring phrase "Then at the sound of the harp, sackbut, psaltery, dulcimer, and all kinds of music" in the story of the three children of Israel in the burning, fiery furnace. They had only the vaguest notions about the instruments in question, and cared less, but the words delighted them.

Reading aloud cannot begin too early. Without thought of what they are doing many mothers begin this process when they sing to their children fragments of old songs, and so lull them to rest. It is nothing to regret if the child goes to sleep under the process. While he is very young, this is perhaps best, for the sound of gentle words becomes linked with the relaxation and security of the twilight hour.

As the child grows older the content of the words becomes of greater importance, for the awakening intelligence demands explanation of terms that are not self-evident and asks some connection with its own existence, or that of its playfellows. Yet even here the charm of faintly understood rhythms and ideas is a potent force in developing that most elusive and valuable gift, an appreciation of literary style.

What to Read

With the littlest children the choice of material for reading aloud should be varied in accordance with a definite plan. Where the aim is specially the development of a love of harmonious speech, as has been suggested above, there is nothing of greater value than poetry, especially poetry with a definite rhythm, a delicately recurring rhyme, or a refrain that serves to unite the several parts. Do not feel it necessary to stick to the idea of using jingles and nonsense verses at this stage. These have their place, but it is not as large a one as is commonly supposed. Such a poem as Jean Inglow's

"High Tide on the Coast of Lincolnshire," with its echoing song and firm measure, will do infinitely more than
an ordinary jingle.

There are, it is true, series of verses, like the famous
Mother Goose rhymes, which bear an exceptional relation to the educational development of the race. For a
child to grow up in ignorance of them would be as un-
thinkable from the standpoint of any rational education
as for him to grow up without the knowledge of how to
use his arms and legs. Mother Goose and kindred flights
of fancy have become a part of the texture of our life,
which we cannot eliminate even if we would. But it
should not be forgotten that these owe their value not to
their inherent quality but to their continued recurrence
in the growth of each generation. Their mastery presents the fewest difficulties to the child mind and consequently involves the least increment.

At the same time these readings may be made fundamental in furthering the child's power of articulate
speech. I remember the quickness with which a child of
less than two years old, who was just beginning to talk,
repeated the "wee, wee, wee" of a familiar nursery
rhyme because the accent of the little piggie's cry
caught his attention. Any oft-repeated sound would
have served as well, as was proved by his efforts to say
the words "by and by" and to combine them with others
of his own choosing. In both cases the imitative faculty
was at work. The importance of reading aloud to very
little children lies in providing something upon which
this imitation may be exercised. When you reflect that
it is by this means that children learn their grammati-
cal or ungrammatical speech, you will appreciate the
incalculable value of the training.

In addition to the sort of material just mentioned, there must be considered the vast body of folklore and fairy literature which has importance of another kind. Here, too, the effect on the habitual speech of the child will be in direct proportion to the excellence of the telling, and a well-told fairy tale has limitless possibilities. I remember a seven-year-old who had read and listened to a translation of the *Odyssey* and who started out upon a version of one of the familiar stories in his own words, in which he referred to the fairy as the "heavenly goddess" after the manner of Homer. The importance of this incident lies in its illustration of the unconscious assimilation of a linguistic point of approach.

It is during this period that tastes are formed, standards are created and comparisons noted for future reference. It is the most fertile period in the development of a real and lasting culture.

From the time he begins to read up to the tenth or twelfth year, the average child is occupied with the acquisition of more or less necessary information. If he is fortunate, he learns to read quickly enough to be able to make use of the books in the family or town library between eight and ten, or earlier in exceptional cases; but the reading is usually far from easy and its subject matter considerably below the child's real intelligence for that reason. It is as soon as this stage is past that the real transition begins.

The transition from childhood to youth is one of the processes that take place so subtly and silently that often the first indication of them is also the knowledge that they are complete. One of the dangers of this period is that the child will get overwhelmed by a mass of inferior material such as is poured out in enormous quantities each year for juvenile consumption. True, the standard literature such as we have been discussing is being outgrown; but this is not the time to substitute indiscriminately selected "girls' books" or "boys' books" to feed the growing intellect. If you have been striving to read only the best literature to your child, it is rather inconsistent to let him read for himself stories which fall far short of the same standard. Juvenile literature there may be, but in as small proportion as possible.

This is the time to begin the interest in the permanent facts of history, of science, of government, of literature and the arts. It is the time to choose the accepted masterpieces of fiction for reading, the great novels of Dickens, of Scott, of Cooper, in order to stimulate as wide a range of interests as possible. Here the mother's duty is largely the invisible one of being able to offer a suggestion at a moment when it may be of service, of guessing the mood of a child's moment and adapting her suggestion to it, of explaining the hard points so that difficulties do not loom mountain-high before the child. Often a sentence or so will suffice to smooth away a difficulty; sometimes the reading aloud of an introductory chapter, a provoking suggestion of excitement to come at a later stage in the book, will be enough to help out the flagging interest and to encourage the process of development.

If the work of the preceding years had been well done, this comes with but little difficulty. The child expects books to be his friends, turns to them naturally, and seeks in them the explanation of things he is anxious to know. He chooses wisely between the good and the best, and his preferences are for the better things. He does not reject the things he does not understand with a contemptuous disdain but pokes into them from time to time, dips into grown-up volumes, and comes back again and again to those that intrigue him. He discards the simpler things with which he has formerly been satisfied and demands more real information. His curiosity is boundless. Everything he reads is the occasion for a question.

These are considerations of vital importance to every mother in choosing books for her children, and while she should make ample allowance for material of immediate interest, she should never forget that the gradual widening of interests is an element which must never be forgotten in her planning.

When to Read

It frequently happens that parents find themselves wholly uncertain as to the best times for reading to the children and for reading by the children themselves. In their anxiety to plan the child's day so that it include the necessary hours of rest, outdoor play and lesson time, both that spent in school and that spent in the preparation of schoolwork, they find no room for reading.

Fortunately, the remedy is a simple one and not far to seek. Have many books lying around where the children can at all times find them, and insist that at the odd moments, such as the half hour before dinner, the intervals between play and meals and the like, the child occupy himself with a book of some sort. Often such occupation will solve two difficult problems at once: the restlessness and mischief that are the result of idleness, and the development of a valuable habit.

This browsing, which the child must do for himself,

is naturally a supplementary part of the home reading aloud. Mothers should remember that children will often enjoy being read to but will not take the pains to read by themselves. Where such a tendency appears it indicates an intellectual laziness that must be checked at once. The best evidence that the home reading aloud has taken its rightful place is that the child is eager to read by himself or to reread the stories which have been read to him.

There are other ends to be served by browsing about among books of various character. The mere reading of titles will often serve to develop curiosity and interest. A child who comes across the name of Napoleon, let us say, blazoned with the imperial crest on the back of an imposing volume, may well be led to ask questions, to look for pictures, and to begin an interest in a real and important historical study.

It is here that the importance of pictures shows itself. Many a child has opened a book, stopped to gaze at the pictures, and then turned to the text in the hope of finding an explanation of the thing which has caught his attention. He may or may not find it, but in the search he is likely to find something of equal interest. The frequent handling of books, even before the mechanical process of reading has been mastered, is one of the great aids to a child's progress.

A wise mother will suggest that the child follow her as she reads, especially the youngster who has partly mastered the art of reading but who stumbles over the polysyllables. A paper cutter which trails over the page helps to guide the child who follows the words, and without special effort the youngster learns to recognize words as they occur and acquires the materials for

guessing correctly in his own reading. It is not necessary
to insist too closely on attention to the text—for, of
course, the exciting passages cannot be interfered with!
—but a measure of attention is worth demanding. To a
very little child, indeed, this process enhances the
magic of the printed page and proves the most effective
stimulus to active reading.

And finally, above all things, plan for a special time
at which the children shall be free to read as they
please, at a time when they need not be driven out of the
house to play, when they need not run and race and
romp, when some quiet occupation is essential, and
when reading is the natural choice. At this time you
may select several promising books and let the child
choose from them that which suits him best, or you may
leave him free to explore the bookshelves. Most of all,
however, give him a time when he can comfortably
read without interruption, and so lay the foundation for
a lifetime habit.

Why Read?

In planning a child's reading, a mother should always
remember that the vast majority of fairy tales have
passed through so many hands in the telling and retell-
ing that their form has often lost its distinctive excellence and their value is restricted to their content.
There are striking exceptions to this rule, as in the
Greek myths retold by Hawthorne in the *Wonder Book*
and *Tanglewood Tales;* but unfortunately the tendency
has been to simplify the telling and to rob it of the
charm of style which it had in the original version. For

this reason the value of most myths and legends lies in their subject matter and their interest for the child—a value which is not to be despised; but a wise mother will not forget this fact and will strive to direct the child's reading to stories in which the sheer interest in the story is coupled with excellence of style.

There is one group of stories especially in which this quality is often lost in the attempt to bring the tales themselves within the limited horizon ascribed to young children. The Bible stories, as they are usually retold for children, lack the charm of style which they possess in eminent degree in their original English form. These, more than any other stories with which I am familiar, have a profound influence upon the spoken and written style of young children. The diction and structure of the sentences, the cadence of the phrasing, and the simplicity and dignity of the telling make a profound impression upon children and do more to foster purity of speech than almost any other single influence. It is therefore of the utmost importance that these should be well known to the child, and known through the medium of the living voice.

The same thing is true of poetry, which depends for its effect so largely upon the sound of its music. The mother need not be afraid to overemphasize the rhythm and cadences here, for the more clearly children appreciate the musical elements in verse, the more they love it. Most of all, however, she should endeavor in her own speech to stress the qualities she wishes the child to copy. Most mothers know how swiftly the tones of a child's voice will show his mental condition. By steadily insisting upon an even, agreeable tone, serious faults of character may often be lessened or corrected.

Such are some of the aims which are to be served by the reading to and with the children—reading which should be made a regular part of every household's life and in which as many of the family members as possible should take part. It will never be forgotten by the children who enjoy it. It will help to bring back one of the lost arts—the art of reading aloud—in which our grandparents were skilled but which a younger generation has discarded.

Too often when children grow up, they find that they have no spiritual kinship with their own families, partly because of diversity of interests but more often because of the separation in pleasures and duties which removes one from contact with the other. The home reading is one of the subtle influences which tends to prevent the growing apart that is the tragedy of so many families.

How to Read

We have spoken of the effect of reading aloud on the linguistic development of the child and of its value in stimulating and encouraging an appreciation of beautiful verbal expression. The necessity for this linguistic development cannot be overemphasized; but in emphasizing it, one should never forget that there is another purpose to be served in the daily reading with the children. This is served by the reading which is designed to open up to them new ranges of experience and acquaintance with the conditions of life, which otherwise they could not gain in so short a time.

There is a very large body of such literature for children. Stories of adventure on land and sea, stories of heroism, stories of strange lands and customs—all these may be called into mind. It may well happen that the story of Franklin's kite may lead to a child's acquaintance with a whole new range of facts of vital importance to his education, or that the interest excited by a tale of a Chinese student may be the steppingstone to geographical knowledge that would otherwise have waited indefinitely.

From this standpoint the body of literature that may profitably be included in the child's acquaintance is indefinitely extended. It includes much that is wholly within the child's range of comprehension, and more that is only partially within his grasp. The swiftness and definiteness of the action, the vigor and movement of the story are the factors that ccmpensate for the maturity which the child does not understand.

17

HOW TO TEACH CONCENTRATION TO CHILDREN

Concentration is a matter of superlative interest in the training of children, because in its acquisition and use lies the success of life. At the basis of concentration lies interest. Let a man stand on the street corner and simply look up into the air, and presently there will be a crowd standing around him looking up and wondering what he is looking at. So it is with the mental attitude. If you are interested, your child will be stimulated to be interested, first because you are. If you make this explanation striking and vivid, you will gain a large fund of interest which will hold out till the time for you to bring forth another striking point. Notice how the newspapers do this. Big events have big headlines. With a child you must always keep in mind that you are dealing first of all in mental headlines. Draw the picture in big outlines. Make the story vivid. Make the contrasts sharp and decisive.

Always deal in clear ideas. Say what you say slowly, remembering that it is important that the child hear the subject matter clearly and grasp the facts. Speak slowly and distinctly. When possible, have the child look directly at you or at the object about which you are speaking. If it is an object, use a pencil or a pointer, always keeping it slightly in motion, so as to keep the eye following it. At the same time keep up enough speed to prevent the wandering of the mind. Don't prolong each exercise above a fair length, but keep on till it is clear that you have made a distinct impression, and then continue again at another time. But see to it that each day, or in each group of two or three days, you have prolonged the period of fixed attention slightly, so that you get a gradual increase in the time required.

It is often well here to use a watch, or to listen to the ticking of a clock and have the child count the ticks slowly. With small children this has often the desired effect, because the mechanism of the watch is itself interesting enough to call for a certain amount of curiosity. And here is another hint. Intellectual curiosity, like every other kind, is stimulated by the gradual rather than by the sudden unfolding of the final result. Come to it gradually, lifting the veil of your narrative slowly so that you increase the wonder as to how it will end.

It will help in this matter of concentration if you use dramatic methods. Changes in the inflection of the voice, use of the face or hands or the arms, or taking sudden postures of the body help here. This is because the eye sees a vivid picture and associates the picture with the idea. A friend of mine uses what he calls the "physiological" method of teaching, by which he means that at important stages he places his finger on his nose in a quizzical way. Then the children know something striking is coming and they watch, while he pauses till every eye is on him and then he lets it go. The children rarely miss the point. Still another device he uses is to raise his eyebrows just before he has something important to communicate.

There are many such little devices associated with

something in the home that may be used. Often I used to say, "The king will now speak!" and then instantly all my children would stop and look up and wait to hear what the king had to say. Every time you make a pause you increase the power of self-inhibition or self-stoppage, which is the beginning of concentration power. Such moments, when they become extended, are the source of mental power.

Another way of getting concentration is to arrange a group of questions bearing upon a single passage, a stanza of a poem, a figure in history, a battle or a picture and make a rapid series of questions that require quick mobilization of the thought on that subject alone. It helps in this method if the object is placed before the child.

The awakening imagination is fed, trained and stimulated early in life by the world's great wonder stories and fairy tales and tales of animal life. Later this is accomplished by true stories of exploration, adventure and invention, and by descriptions of our wonderful world and its relation to mankind. Finally it receives its highest development and culture by continuing a familiarity throughout life with poetry, music, drama and the fine arts.

18

THE USE OF PICTURES

To the undeveloped mind the earliest appeal comes from pictures, which convey the imagination of another in a concrete form rather than in words, which are necessarily less definite in their expression. This is why children turn instinctively to books with many pictures, and from the pictures to the text rather than from the text to the pictures. They can understand the picture more readily than the text, and it is the natural characteristic of the mind to adopt the easiest means of gaining the information it seeks.

It follows, then, that the pictures a child sees are among the earliest formative influences on the growing imagination. The story of Sir Galahad, for example, means far less to a child who has never seen the picture than it does to the boy or girl who remembers the noble head of the white horse and the boyish face of the knight. It is possible to describe the armor of a knight with care and detail and have it mean not a single thing to the child, whereas even a poor picture suggests and explains completely. This was the psychology behind the constant attempts of men to represent their divinities, which led to the marvelous succession of Greek marbles and to the no less remarkable Christian Madonnas.

The earliest possible cultivation of the imagination, therefore, begins with the choice of pictures which, by their suggested action, their coloring, their detail, excite interest and curiosity. Using these as a basis a mother may open up to her child great spaces of intellectual interest and may lay the foundation for permanent interests. She must be sure not only that the child is amply provided with pictures but also that his questions are answered as they occur and that his attention is called to the essential elements of the work. Fortunately, there are many famous pictures which deal with subjects that occur constantly in a child's daily and imaginative life and which may be used to stimulate that life.

As a child grows older he can be taught to look more and more closely at the genuine artistic values that a picture displays and be taught to discriminate between the true and false forms of art. Now is the time to call his attention to the composition and design of the pictures which have already made their appeal to his interest and to show the innumerable ways in which the artist's skill is exhibited. It is surprising how even a young child will perceive the essential merits and defects of a picture if he has no perverted judgments to begin with.

One of the favorite ways in which imagination may be directly stimulated is that of inventing a story to fit a picture. I remember with delight the story an eight-year-old built around a somber etching of moorland and wintry evening, which suggested mainly a mood and an atmosphere. This is, indeed, the central aim of the largest part of modern art, the suggestion of thoughts and fancies which take their point of departure from the picture, though not necessarily related to it.

19

THE VALUE OF MUSIC

The second great appeal to the imagination of children is that made by music. It is a matter of common comment that even the youngest little ones are enchanted by the harmony of songs and will listen for hours to music—good, bad, or indifferent—if they have the chance. Not only does music appeal to their senses in this fashion but it also suggests far wider matters. The child learns to hear the beat of the horse's hoofs in the sound of the instrument, and in the process he begins to invent stories for himself, explanations that start from the melody and wind up in the realm of fairyland with which his stories have already made him familiar. He is exercising the faculties of imagination that offer the greatest hope of mental growth.

A wise mother will make the fullest use of modern aids in stimulating this side of her child's nature. If there is a reproducing machine of any sort in the house, she will endeavor to have the child enjoy it as often and as long as possible. She will endeavor to guide his interest away from the gaudy and meretricious popular music and will give him the opportunity to become familiar with the great music of the world, choosing themes in accordance with his growing capacity to enjoy them. From the simple ballad music and the familiar folk songs and dances, she will pass by regular degrees to more complicated music, taking the single precaution of never continuing too long at a single time to strain the attention of the child.

20

THE INFLUENCE OF DRAMA

The drama has always held a position of special distinction in its relation to the imagination of the race. It was the first great instrument of instruction and communication of ideas in a time when men had none of the aids in making their thoughts known to each other that they now have. Dramas which could formerly be seen only in the large cities are now translated into the motion-picture film, which travels everywhere at slight expense. There is no longer any reason why any child should be deprived of the imaginative increment which the stage gives. This increment is of two sorts. In part it comes from the new ideas that are introduced by the subject matter of a play, and in part from the sheer beauty of production, which visualizes so much for the child mind. The parent must make serious and thoughtful selection from among the possible productions for his child to witness. First choice of all is, naturally, the great body of classic English drama, which is all too seldom performed on our stage. When this is not possible, the wise use of motion-picture opportunities is to be recommended. In answering all the questions that arise in this connection, the parent must be guided by his or her own best judgment of the particular child. Some children are more sensitive than others to special subjects. With some, the visualizing of a favorite story—say *Treasure Island*—will have the effect of preventing them from reading the book—a result which should at all costs be avoided. For others it may give the necessary incentive to the accomplishment of a difficult task. There is no possible rule in the matter, save the simple one of the excellence, beauty and general fitness of the production.

It must never be forgotten that the stimulus of the stage is largely on the visual side, especially for children, and that while it expands the imaginative faculties on the one hand, it also contracts them by limiting them in their range. This is the reason why the educational value of the stage is, on the whole, limited to rather older children. It is well to keep the theater in the realm of high and special pleasures until the child is well past the ten-year mark, at least.

There was a time in American home life, before the day of vast institutions and enormous educational machinery, when the home was the greatest training center in the land. Parents knew that unless they took a deep personal interest in the work and education of their children, the children would not receive the mental equipment necessary for usefulness and success in life. They had no alternative but to take this as part of the business of being parents.

Then there followed the vast development which we see today, and, singular as it may seem, in the greatness of our educational expansion we have arrived at exactly the same place as we were before; but this time it is because our public institutions have grown so large that the child is more often than not completely submerged by them.

Thus we are coming back to where we were at the beginning: whereas once the home had to take a vigorous interest in the development and training of the child because the facilities were few and poor, now we must do the same thing because the numbers are so great, the teachers are so relatively few and the task of teaching great numbers in a single group almost impossible.

No teacher can do this as well as the parent, if indeed the teacher can do it at all. In a group of forty or fifty children, or even in a smaller group of twenty, if your child gets all that he is entitled to, he will only get one twentieth of the time and strength of the teacher. How can we expect both intellectual training and character-building to be developed in that fraction of one teacher's time and strength? And if there is a disturbance or failure on the part of any one of the twenty, he gets even less than his twentieth!

The home is the greatest school of life and the parent is the greatest teacher in the world. For teach we must, my friend, whether we will or not; if we do it intelligently and according to a plan, we make great strides for ourselves and for our children. If we neglect them on this side of their life, we are nevertheless teaching them —by our neglect. It is therefore our great opportunity to give the initial emphasis and the earliest inspirations out of which subsequent life and character emerge.

IV
BERLE TODAY

21

IN TERMS OF MODERN THEORY

Modern educators and psychologists, although still somewhat inexact in their conclusions about the human brain, present convincing evidence that intelligence can be increased if proper conditions are created to foster growth. As we shall see later in this chapter the Berle Primer, with incredible prescience, sets out a distillation of methods that have support in a variety of scholarly quarters. But first, the evidence in support of the contention that intelligence is susceptible to induced growth:

A clue, unscientific in the manner in which the data was collected but impressive because of the nature of the subject, may be found in the private papers of Albert Einstein, which were published for the first time in 1972. They confirmed the popular legend that Einstein had been a poor student. The highly regimented system of education that prevailed in nineteenth-century Germany frustrated the boy's native talents. The intellectual sparks of Einstein's youth, reported in his writings and those of his sister, Maja, seemed trivial: mathematical puzzles posed by his uncle, Jakob Einstein; a model steam engine given by another uncle, Casar Koch; a geometry book which he enjoyed perusing; a compass given to him when he was four by his father. This is the stuff of which genius is made.

A more scientific study confirms the idea suggested by the Einstein papers: certain conditions of the home tend to encourage, perhaps create, genius. Dr. Harold G. McCurdy of the University of North Carolina probed the childhood patterns of twenty "historical geniuses" whose early years were well documented. He found a number of factors common to all of his subjects: a high degree of attention focused on the child by parents and other adults, "expressed in intensive educational matters and, usually, abundant love"; careful monitoring of material presented to the child, especially from sources outside the family; and "a rich efflorescence of fantasy." All echoes of Berle.

The most impressive insight into expansion of human intelligence comes not from a review of geniuses, however, but from the other end of the intellectual spectrum. In 1938 Professor Harold Sheels and other University of Iowa psychologists conducted a study of thirteen infants with a mean IQ of 64.3 and a range between 36 and 89 who were transferred to a school for the mentally retarded from an orphanage in which they had been given no special treatment. They were placed in a ward with brighter children of all ages and attentive adults. Thereafter, they were periodically retested. Each of the thirteen showed a gain in IQ—from a minimum of 7 points to a maximum of 58, all but four showing gains of more than 20 points. Twelve other young inmates had been left in the orphanage; their IQs were considerably higher, with a mean of 87 and a range from 50 to 103. When these infants were later retested, they showed a decrease in IQ of from 8 to 45 points, with five exceeding 35 points.

Twenty-one years later all of these cases were relocated. The results were striking. The thirteen who had been given intensive treatment at the school for the mentally retarded were all self-supporting. Eleven had been adopted and none were in wards of any institution. All but two were married, nine of these with children. The twelve children left in the orphanage revealed a different, sorry record: one died in a state institution during adolescence and five others were still wards of state institutions at the time of the survey. Of the six who were not institutionalized, only two had married and one of those had divorced. The survey also traced the educational record of both groups. The median grade completed by the thirteen children given special treatment at the school for the mentally retarded was the twelfth (i.e., high-school graduates). Four had gone on to one or more years of college, one graduating. Of the twelve who remained at the orphanage, six failed to complete third grade and none graduated from high school. It is important to note that the age range of the thirteen infants who were transferred to the school for the mentally retarded was from seven to thirty months. The significant gains were made in the years before formal schooling would normally begin.

According to one observer, Harold Skeels and his colleagues "were very nearly drummed out of the American Psychological Association" when they presented their original study in 1938. Their conclusions were simply too much at odds with the doctrinaire view at that time that intelligence was an inherited trait. Skeels did *not* know that Dr. Berle had made a similar study, forming similar conclusions (albeit based more on intuition than detailed scientific analysis) some three decades earlier. In the third edition of his basic text, Berle reviewed a lengthy report of a Massachusetts State commission which attributed entry into prostitu-

tion in large measure to the feeblemindedness of the
prostitutes. Berle noted that his own studies had found
many institutions scattered throughout the land in
which intensive cultivation had led to "increased mental power" in the feebleminded. He then asked, "Suppose we gave normal, healthy children the same attention that we give to the feebleminded?" In a sense this
was the theoretical justification of the Berle method.

Other studies support the premise upon which Berle's
work was based: scores from tests administered in the
preschool years show little relationship to tests administered to the same panel during adolescence; substantial differences have been found in the IQs of identical
twins reared apart; children placed in foster homes
have demonstrated superior performance to those left
in old-fashioned orphanages.

Still the debate rages as to whether intelligence can
be increased or is simply a function of genes. Berkeley
professor Arthur R. Jensen is widely cited for the proposition that heredity is dispositive of intelligence. Actually, Jensen views environment as a "threshold vari-
able" and admits that it may account for some 30
percent of human intelligence. Even so, his thesis seems
to put human beings in a lower category than frogs and
rats and pet-reared dogs, all of whom show a considerable improvement over parallel numbers if proper
treatment is received in the early days of their lives.

It seems clear that human intelligence may be expanded. Having accepted this basic premise, it remains
to examine in some detail the locale of the Berle method
—the home—and the optimum subject for the use of the
method, the preschool child. In doing so, we shall see
that each of Berle's methods is supported in terms of
modern theory.

Two Reservations

Upon first discovering *Self Culture* some five years
ago, two reservations came to my mind, which I have
since resolved to my own satisfaction. For what it is
worth, and because these reservations will undoubtedly
occur to the present readers, I pass these doubts and my
personal resolution of them on to you before proceeding
to review Berle within the context of modern theory. My
first concern was with the advisability in terms of emotional and social development of sending children to
college three or four years early—even assuming increased knowledge and intelligence. My second question was the question of whether methods developed
over fifty years ago could have utility today. And the
corollary question: If Berle's works were so valuable,
why had they totally disappeared from the scene?

THE CONSEQUENCES OF EARLY ADMISSION. Early admission
of the Berle children to Harvard and Radcliffe was not
a part of the Berle method but a result of it. It was
important to Dr. Berle, of course, because it proved the
effectiveness of the method. But it may have had a nega-
tive effect on his teaching—long after the preschool
phase—because it introduced an element of objective-
orientation in pointing for the college entrance exams
that is at odds with normal pursuit of the Berle method.
There would appear to be no reason to send children to
college ahead of their chronological peer groups, with
the attendant social problems which could result, so
long as the material the children receive in school continues to challenge their advanced intelligence and
knowledge. If early attendance at college becomes the

norm, and accelerated programs are now receiving attention at many institutions of higher learning, then social or emotional problems would be minimized. In any event, the responsibility in this area of modern parents is fully anticipated in the primer set out in these pages: parents must work closely with teachers to enhance the fare offered in primary and secondary schools; they must insist on classrooms where young children can learn advanced material with and from older children; and parents must constantly seek to enrich the intellectual atmosphere of the home.

AN UNREASONABLE DISAPPEARANCE. Three of the most influential works in modern educational theory were published half a century ago. Maria Montessori's *The Montessori Method* was first published in English in 1912, and John Dewey's *Interest and Effort in Education* appeared in 1913. Jean Piaget was initially published in book form in 1926 in *The Language and Thought of the Child.* This is not to say that each of these works is fully accepted by modern educators. Each author has energetic advocates and detractors. Today Montessori schools are among the most advanced—some say too advanced. The British infant schools, of which more will be written later in this chapter, stem in large measure from Dewey's pioneer work at the Francis Parker School in Chicago, although Britons prefer to give credit to British educators, such as Susan Isaacs and the McMillan sisters. Of course, almost every discussion about curriculum development for young children evokes an enthusiastic affirmation or attack on Piaget.

The School and the Home enjoyed success when first published. Although Berle's *Self Culture* did not have equal popularity, it is, as we have seen, extremely useful as a guide to implementing the principles developed in the companion book. Most likely, two completely unrelated public attitudes led to Berle's complete disappearance as an influence on the American educational scene.

First, widespread use of the IQ and achievement tests appeared for the first time in World War I. The Alpha and Beta intelligence tests led to a belief in fixed intelligence, which made Berle's work seem entirely useless. The intelligence-testing movement led to a decline of interest in Maria Montessori's ideas as well as Berle's. What a grotesque irony that an exaggerated test-consciousness should destroy the public interest in methods which had demonstrated that a child's intelligence could be increased! It was more likely a second factor, however, which inhibited continuing public acceptance of Berle's books: Berle frequently praised German schools and techniques at a time, during and immediately after World War I, when the American mood was distinctly anti-German. For whatever reason, after a decade on the American scene, in which *The School and the Home* went through six printings and three editions, the influence of Dr. Adolf A. Berle, Sr. almost completely disappeared.

Berle's methods, though proven, were so unique and innovative that widespread implementation might have been impossible fifty years ago. Today we stand at what may be a revolution in American education, centering largely on the development of the mind of the preschool child. And from many quarters the methods developed by Dr. Berle so long ago have, at last, gained solid academic support.

The Woods Hole Conference

In September, 1959, some thirty-five scientists, scholars and educators gathered at Woods Hole on Cape Cod to discuss how the teaching of science might be improved in primary and secondary schools. After the conference a report of its proceedings, a "sense of the meeting," was prepared by Professor Jerome Bruner, the distinguished Harvard psychologist, and published under the title *The Process of Education*. Although the conference was concerned almost entirely with matters dealing with children in school and not with preschool children, it presented, nevertheless, a striking reaffirmation of the principles set out in *The School in the Home*.

Jerome Bruner's book begins by stressing the need for developing an understanding in students of the fundamental *structure* of whatever subjects are taught. As Dr. Bruner points out, "A good theory is the vehicle not only for understanding a phenomenon now, but also for remembering it tomorrow." Note how similar this is to Berle's insistence that parents "create and maintain programs for coordination of the knowledge gained." Of course, Berle has referred to this process as mental fertilization and frequently recalls the need for establishing structure, in such words as "generalizations" and "fundamental relations," and the need for "classification and retention of knowledge" and "mental self-organization." Once having established the basic structure, Bruner notes the ease of transferring information from the specific to the more general and from one field to another, points that Berle makes again and again. Another basic Berle theme which gained affirmation at the Woods Hole conference was the idea, to use Berle's phrases, that "children who 'played' at knowledge" during their early years might find themselves "face to face with the 'science' of the same things at college." Professor Bruner talks about this kind of pattern as "spiral curriculum" in which fundamental material is taught the child at one point in his life and then built on at later points in his education.

There are so many striking parallels between Bruner and Berle that to investigate all of them here would be to repeat both books. The reason for this parallelism may stem from an article of faith which pervades the work of both men. Berle puts it this way: "Almost any child will take up almost any kind of material and assimilate it," and Bruner states it thus: "Any subject can be taught effectively in some intellectually honest form to any child at any stage of development."

The Head Start Experience

The most impressive body of data on the effect of education on children in the three-to-six-year-old age bracket may be found in the records of Operation Head Start. About 470,000 preschool children from disadvantaged homes now take part in this project, which is funded and operated pursuant to guidelines promulgated by the federal government. Since Head Start maintains an office with the special responsibility of evaluating its progress and programs, a wealth of material has been gathered over the past few years. Two studies are germane to the present inquiry. First, in 1968 Marguerite Bittner and others published a study which concluded that children who had participated in Head Start for a full year did better in standard tests (e.g., Preschool Inventory and Metropolitan Reading tests) than first graders who had not had this training. The finding of the Bittner study which received the most publicity, however, was that this initial superior performance of full-year preschool children was not maintained, and that no significant differences existed at the end of the first-grade year between those who had and those who had not participated in Head Start. There was a glimmer of hope in the Bittner study: the children with the best test performances were those whose parents participated in the programs. A second study by Theron Alexander and Margaret Faust confirmed that sustained improvement through the first-grade year was possible where there was greater cooperation of parents. In 1971 the federal government demonstrated its confidence in these findings by establishing a modestly funded program called Home Start, in which Head Start initial services would be performed at home, with the direct involvement of parents in the educational development of their children.

The current debate on federal preschool child care turns on the amount of "enrichment" which should be included in the program and on whether the massive federal funding which would be necessary to establish centers throughout the country is economically feasible. Even while this debate continues, however, data presently available from Operation Head Start indicate that significant gains can be achieved in the home. The Berle program can be instituted by millions of parents at a minimal personal expense, and the results, as we have seen, can be immense.

Piaget's Contribution

We gain much greater understanding as to how and why the Berle method works from the research of the great Swiss psychologist Jean Piaget. Specifically, as it relates to Berle, Piaget's work in "stages of learning" tells us *what* the preschool child can be taught, and his concept of "gating and storage" provides significant insight into *how* children learn.

Piaget has divided the young person's learning process into distinct but sometimes overlapping stages: in early infancy the child seeks to develop an "integrated object concept" by establishing through trial and error a permanent framework for himself and the objects around him, a process that frequently involves picking up all sorts of things and, inevitably, placing them in his mouth; in the preschool years the child's major cognitive task is the mastery of quantitative relations, leading to enthusiasm for such numerically orientated fairy tales as *Goldilocks and the Three Bears* and *The Three Little Pigs;* preadolescents engage in syllogistic reasoning; and finally, in adolescence, the young person begins to deal with abstractions, seeking to master and reflect upon his own thoughts.

While Berle would probably agree with Piaget's concept of a progression of learning plateaus, he would protest the rigidity with which many child-development experts regard these plateaus. Specifically, Berle believed that the rate at which abilities mature is by no means predetermined. Muriel Beadle shares this view, in *A Child's Mind,* in the following terms: "Although one's physical inheritance determines the sequence in which various abilities emerge, the speed at which they develop, and maybe the form, can be profoundly affected by the learning opportunities present in the environment." Jerome Bruner also endorses the possibility of acceleration when he says that "the child is no clockwork sequence of events; he also responds to influences from the environment."

Berle believed that the child controls to a large extent his own ability to proceed from one stage to another or to master the objectives within a stage. Thus, an infant whose mind will not accept the enormous stimulation of a three-ring circus may focus his attention on popcorn or hot dogs. And the baby who is unable to assimilate large numbers of adults may manifest a fear of strangers. This process is called gating. It means, in the words of child psychologist David Elkind, that "the child can elect (a) to keep incoming stimulation from registering or (b) to allow the stimulation to register but delay reaction until all of the information can be adequately assimilated." This latter aspect of gating involves the corollary process of storage. Thus the child who went to the three-ring circus might spontaneously start to draw tigers three or four months later. These reappearing tigers are not wholly without mystery, however, since less is known about the storage process than the stages of learning and the child's ability to pace his own intellectual growth.

It was Berle's genius to perceive that a child possessed a built-in mechanism, since identified by Piaget as the process of gating and storage, which could prevent harm to the child's psyche if the learning process was accelerated and expanded. The unique contribution of the Berle method was to recognize that an early infusion of advanced material in the home could actually increase the intelligence of the properly motivated child.

It is interesting to see how Berle anticipated Piaget's theory. Berle stated that at times a child would appear reluctant to receive any information but that, properly stimulated, "the child will usually do the rest and supply the natural suggestion for the next step in any given direction." He believed that this process could be accelerated, that children's interests "can be widened, their abilities made stronger and their selective habits clarified—all along the line." He recognized, perhaps intuitively, that there were things which "stirred the mind and stored the memory of things that were intellectually fertilizing and distinctly valuable," that proper instruction created "permanent furnishings of the child's mind, which could be stored up for the many varied uses." Berle referred to the framework for storage as "mental organization" or "mental self-organization," a variation, perhaps, of Bruner's notion of structure in that it could be self-defining. Berle saw that what the child organized himself "is his very own and constitutes his reserve stock of mental power for the grasp and attack of new things."

While imagination could open the mind, Berle knew that significant storage was possible only if teaching cut across narrow subject lines. This interdisciplinary approach is a central theme of Berle's. It is also on the crest of modern thinking and leads one to another great debate brewing in American education.

Should the Classroom Be Open or Closed?

If great insight has been gained in recent years as to how children, particularly young children, learn, there is still a considerable difference of informed opinion on the manner in which materials should be presented to children. The polar positions in this controversy are found in the views of advocates of "open" and "closed" education.

Berle would seem to have the best of both of these worlds. At first his method appears to be "closed"—that is, somewhat well ordered and programmed. There is a real kinship apparent between the Berle home school and the classic modern closed model that Bereiter and Engelmann established at the University of Illinois: both seek to operate in a no-nonsense, well-disciplined atmosphere; both emphasize formal structural aspects of language.

But the Berle method has a great deal in common, as well, with the British infant schools that are causing so much comment in educational circles today. Thus the World of Inquiry School, an "open" prototype established by Dr. Elkind in Rochester, New York, shares a number of features with its British counterparts and with Berle, including self-pacing, extensive focus on problem solving and utilization of multi-age rooms. Like these models, the Berle method is relatively free of a highly structured daily curriculum. (Paradoxically, in contrast to American schools, the only content requirement in the British primary system is a corporate act of worship at the beginning of each day.)

One of the reasons that Berle finds support in these divergent schools of education is the locale of his method—the home. Here is an area where the multi-age room is a fact, not a contrivance. Here, as Joseph Featherstone has observed in open classrooms everywhere, "Children learn from each other." Interdisciplinary teaching, which often demands meticulous coordination in the classroom, is a natural condition at home. The dialogue between "teacher" and "student" and among the "students" themselves flows easily at, say, the dinner table. Berle's achievement was to perceive and utilize the assets which the home affords in the process of learning.

Dr. Berle decried the tendency in conventional schools—still prevalent today—to seek the "right" answers that will satisfy the instructors but will soon be forgotten. When John Holt asks in *How Children Fail,* "Are we trying to turn out intelligent people, or test-takers?" he is echoing Berle's denunciation, made fifty years earlier, of schools which are content to teach "ready-made materials for passing examinations." Again, Berle points out the advantage of his chosen locale for teaching: "Questioning in the home takes on the aspect of a search for truth as distinguished from mere accuracy." Of course, this is a principal objective of the open classroom.

In a report on recent developments in British infant schools, Vincent Rogers commends "the eagerness of teachers to cut across disciplinary lines" by focusing on the many different aspects which a given problem presents, such as art, music, poetry, science and history. He refers to these as "lifelike questions," as opposed to those which are narrowly academic. This is exactly

what Berle had in mind when he wrote that "the important thing is to get the mental touch which links the
question to the interests, the personality of the child,
and which admits of the utilization of previous knowledge and inquiry." Berle's lament that "children rarely
apply the principles learned in one sphere of inquiry to
the problems of another" has been overcome in large
measure by the methods of the open classroom.

Berle's insistence that advanced material should be
taught to preschool children is still not widely accepted
by educators—Jerome Bruner is a prominent exception
—but the methods he uses to ensure acceptance of this
material by young children find support in both the
open and closed disciplines. Berle teaches that all
knowledge is a function of *language,* a basic premise of
the closed school, and he knows that it is not necessary
for the child to have the ability to read for himself or to
possess the physical skills needed to read for himself or
to write in order to understand material that is frequently thought to be beyond the ability of the small
child. He is emphatic in his belief that "the serious,
abiding principles of human knowledge may be implanted at a period when most people still indulge in
baby talk with their little ones," and he vigorously op-
poses the notion that this instruction will somehow
spoil the child. "Not a single reason can be adduced," he
contends, "to show that giving a child information
about geometry is one whit more calculated to break
down health than to give him Mother Goose rhymes."
Berle achieves "the habits of attention and concentration" necessary to absorb this advanced material
largely through skillful use of the child's imagination.
His utilization of games or play is a hallmark of the
open classroom.

Even from this brief review of Berle's principal points of emphasis in the light of modern theories of education, it appears clear that Berle is in accord with the best contemporary educational thought, whether the methods advocated are thought of as "open" or "closed." Oddly enough, many of the things he wrote about a half century ago are being "discovered" today. Systematic instruction for the preschool child and insistence that parents be involved in educational programs are points which have only recently gained acceptance. Berle's rationale for using the home as the locale for teaching, with its natural multi-age grouping and its inevitable reduction in child-adult ratio as compared to the classroom, is on the crest of contemporary thinking. His contention that language is the key, that games can be made a significant teaching tool, that books should surround children in random profusion, that the child's question should be the starting point and that the teacher's answers to these questions should cut across many different disciplines are all points which are being presented today as in the forefront of "modern" educational programs.

22

CONTEMPORARY PRACTICE OF THE BERLE METHOD

Even if the Berle method is viewed as fundamentally sound, many parents will ask whether they are skilled enough to use it in the home. After all, teaching is a demanding profession, generally requiring years of college and graduate school before its practitioners can even enter the classroom in the role of instructor. In recent years closed-circuit television, educational films, teaching machines and other paraphernalia have become integral parts of the complex apparatus of teaching. Berle would undoubtedly argue that in the preschool years elaborate equipment is generally unnecessary. He would contend that parents possess an advantage, especially in the comfortable, natural surroundings of the home, that other teachers, with years of technical training, simply do not have. And Berle could point to accomplishments with his own students so astounding that few teachers could make equal claims. Finally, he could demonstrate that his methods are so simple and the results so immediately apparent in the child that almost any parent can quickly learn to use the Berle method to the satisfaction and enjoyment of children and parent alike.

Creating an Atmosphere of Excellence

The Berle method is thoroughly described in this book and does not need elaborate restatement here. In a later portion of this chapter, entitled "Walden Three," the method can be seen in action through various specific illustrative uses. Here a few words will suffice to suggest how modern parents can create the atmosphere in which the method can be most productive, touching on four key points: the home, use of the family group, the inquiry method and the importance of play. All of these add up to "enrichment," a word that Adolf Berle, Sr., first used in this connection in 1912.

THE POWER OF THE HOME. As we have seen, the home possesses certain unique advantages as a locale for education that are extremely difficult to obtain elsewhere. The natural unity that prevails in the home admits of no fragmentation of subjects or instructors. Values mightily strived for in other settings, in both open and closed classrooms, are natural in the home. In *Education and Ecstasy* George Leonard notes that an outspoken and successful group of modern educators have based their approach on the following premise: "Practically everything that is *presently* being accomplished in the schools can be accomplished more effectively and with less pain in the average child's home and neighborhood playground." One of these educators, Dr. M. W. Sullivan, finds traditional schools entirely disruptive of true education and suggests that a child sitting at home with a tape recorder, a foot pedal and a simple written program telling him how and when to play the tapes would be better off than children are in today's schools.

Berle's warning that theater—where the stimulus was "largely on the visual side"—should be strictly rationed for young children would appear to apply directly to television. His lament that travel is not available for young children is no longer as true as it was at the beginning of the century. Today, family travel can be a stimulating part of a child's education. But generally speaking, the advantages of the home and the attendant disadvantages found in the conventional educational system are, surprisingly, almost the same today as they were fifty years ago.

It is not difficult to see that the traditional school appears almost designed to frustrate the factors that produce genius. But it would be unfair not to admit that the traditional home can easily have the same frustrating effect. If parents ignore their children or, even worse, fill the young minds with wasteful material and bad habits, the natural advantages of the home are not only lost but turned against the child. The parent, having recognized that the early years are the ideal time to start on education and that the home represents an optimum setting, must proceed to use the methods that will produce the most desirable results.

THE FAMILY GROUP. Once the parent is aware that the home provides countless instances to increase the knowledge of the child and the child's own ability to learn, the advantages of utilizing this process on "family" occasions can immediately be seen. Mealtime was such an event in the Berle home. The author's description is worth quoting at length: "The silver at the table, the glass, the food and its sources, all become the

media for the conveying of exact and interesting knowledge. Now the important thing about all these things
was not merely that real and useful information was
placed in the mind, but that the mind itself was being
fertilized for the subsequent reception of other information and provided with the machinery for its proper
classification and retention. In this way geography and
arithmetic and grammar and various sciences were
taught not as such but as fertilizing material which by
their occupancy of the mind excluded the vile stuff that
is usually doled out to the infant intellect. What is more,
and perhaps best of all, is that these particular children
were made immune from the misuse of their minds
later on in life." Decades later the Berle children
remembered these occasions with fondness. They recalled that the advanced nature of the material actually
increased their pleasure. Mealtime was interesting and
eagerly awaited. Dullness and routine gave way to
lively discussion.

If there are a number of children in the family or
there are older guests at the table, it is important to note
that the adult's view does not always have to prevail. It
might be that the child will dispute the parent's exposi-
tion and present his own ideas in a lively discussion. In
the Berle family the father maintained control and respect even when the encyclopedia proved him to be
"wrong" on a given point. Respect for scholarship must
always be preserved, however.

Berle emphasized the importance of youthful expression and gave the example of "The Story," in which
each child in the Berle nursery, before going to sleep,
took a turn in adding a chapter to a narrative that continued for a number of years. This is the classic "multi-

age situation" about which current educators are so enthusiastic. Older children teach younger ones, by design
or example. In the course of expressing himself and in
answering the questions of the other children the child
is developing his mental self-organization, his framework for retaining knowledge, and thereby increasing
his ability to learn.

The elements of discipline and reward must be carefully reviewed in the context of the family group. Initially, as Berle points out, proper habits of concentration
and order must be instilled in the children. This training of the will often involves a discipline more rigid
than that generally applied by parents to children in the
average home. However, Berle insists that the discipline must be reasonable and related to the goal sought.
Also, he notes that after this sense of order has been
established the child develops a true happiness in the
learning process. A large measure of this happiness
comes from the inherent joy of learning and the manner in which imagination is skillfully used to motivate
the child. Another important factor is the parent's ap-
probation. Behaviorists call this element "positive rein-
forcement." A favorable climate can be further enhanced if the child is led to expect that he will do well.
This element of "self-fulfilling prophecy" can be found
in an ironic context in some school systems. Bright children are segregated into special groups. Surveys now
indicate that many times they do well *because they are
led to believe that they will do well.* (This thesis has led
Postman and Weingartner to suggest in *Teaching as a
Subversive Activity* that teachers in traditional classroom settings might get more out of their students if
they promised all of them *A*'s at the beginning of the

course.) Such productive encouragement (which Berle discusses under the heading of "breeding intellectual ambition") can be most easily established by building on the natural love and mutual desire to please that prevails in the family.

The basic advantages that stem from the proper exploitation of the family group may have an even greater relevance today than they did in Berle's time. Absentee fathers and working mothers are far more common now than in 1900. It is important to note that the Berle method does *not* require a great deal of parental time: the quality of the time is important. Also, other members of the family teach, decreasing the demand on the parent's attention. Finally, by instilling habits of attention and intellectual interest during the preschool period, the parent is easing the burden of later years. The Berle method is not a miracle cure for urban ills, but at the very least it can be seen to alleviate desperate problems that have been viewed as almost without solution. THE INQUIRY METHOD. The inquiry method, with its attendant emphasis on language, is at the very heart of Berle. This is not a matter of mere form. Postman and Weingartner make clear their belief in the substantial importance of this point as follows: "The art and science of asking questions is the source of all knowledge."

If the child's question, indicating as it does a personal interest in the subject at hand, can be used as the point of departure, then so much the better. This book does not contemplate a parental obligation to develop an elaborate educational program for preschool children. What Berle suggests is that the normal events of childhood can be greatly enhanced if the parent will take the time to utilize these events to maximize the child's edu-

cational experience. Berle calls this process "fertilization of the mind," and the occasion for its use might be
a trip to the zoo by a child with his friends or a matter
in the current news which the parents are discussing at
the dinner table or a movie or a television show which
the child has just seen. This *does* require some small
preparation by the parent. Most often the information
will be imparted to the child as a result of a question
asked by the child (but easily anticipated by the parent).
As Berle says, the process "involves the cultivation in
the home of the art of questioning and of answering
questions and of interlinking factual knowledge with
inferential judgments so as to make available whatever
knowledge there is in the child's mind." Advanced
materials can be imparted to the child mind, and the
child, with his questions and expressions, will set the
pace. But these opportunities are meaningless unless
the parent is prepared to use them.

If the adult is initiating the questioning, he must bear
in mind that his objective is not only to impart knowledge to the child but also to try to expand the child's
mind by challenging it. Thus, simple questions such as
"What do you worry about the most?" "What bothers you
the most about adults?" "Why?" "How can you tell 'good
guys' from 'bad guys'?" (to borrow some random questions from Postman and Weingartner) are the kind of
fare which the small child can enjoy and which will
stimulate his thinking. Frequently, the adult's questions
will center upon language, which Berle has recognized
as the key to learning. This involves more, of course,
than just the study of correct usage. In the course of
viewing words as symbols and examining their sounds,
one discovers new dimensions of language and, in the

process, of thought. The medium is, indeed, the message. Here Berle is in the forefront of modern educational experimenters. He would point out, however, that it is not necessary for a man to be a skilled philologist in order to instruct his children in this complex area. All that is needed is a sense of inquiry and examination. More than anything else, it is the *attitude* of inquiry that holds each word up to scrutiny and fills the mental computer, the brain, with stuff which, for one reason or another, tends to expand and increase its content.

It is instructive here to review the materials and equipment on which Berle relies. In the main, four materials were used to carry out his teaching in the home: the dictionary, examples from nature, the Bible and the encyclopedia.

Berle believed that the dictionary should be used as more than a source for checking the accuracy of language. He found that stories could be told by examining the nature of word roots. As a corollary to this he had the children memorize passages of Greek and Latin, even though they did not know those languages. He wanted them to enjoy the sound of language. We find numerous examples throughout Berle of the use of nature as a material for instruction: a worm becomes the point of departure for a discussion of the meaning of *species,* and water coursing through the garden provides an opportunity to discuss erosion.

Berle's use of the Bible undoubtedly stemmed from his background as a minister. However, he points out that it is also a splendid piece of English literature and a doorway to many other areas of knowledge. Berle suggests the need for embellishment and historical illustration to Biblical narrative, but emphasizes the impor-

tance of exposing the child to the richness of traditional
Biblical language. The first volume of *Self Culture* included a number of classical Biblical stories from both
the Old and the New Testament for reading aloud to
small children. These were somewhat modernized, ab-
breviated excerpts of the King James version, with an
apparent effort by Berle to retain as much richness of
language as was consonant with enjoyment by a young
child. Modern treatment, such as Pearl Buck's *Story Bible,* would suffice at this stage. As the child grows older,
the original text might be used for greater value in linguistic training.

The encyclopedia can be used in a number of ways. It
can become an aid by which parents will be able to
prepare a brief factual background in anticipation of
questions which might be asked by children at the dinner table or at some special event, such as a television
program set in an interesting period of history; it can be
used as an arbitrator or reference when disputes arise
in family discussions; and, finally, as the children grow
older they will refer to the encyclopedia, and primary
sources, as their own basis of information. Berle recalls
that his children learned to play chess by reading about
the game in the encyclopedia and instructing each
other. Almost any standard encyclopedia can be substituted for *Self Culture* if used in conjunction with selected additional materials. Fairy tales; adventure stories; nature studies; accounts of travel and invention;
introductions to drama, music and the arts; and biographies of "great men and women" were all included in
Self Culture. For the most part they are brief treat-
ments, sparking the intellectual curiosity of the child,
providing what Whitehead once described as "an expo-

sure to greatness." Illustrations and photographs were frequent. Books containing this information can easily be obtained, and they are probably more convenient to use in separate volumes than they were as segments of *Self Culture*.

Some parents might want to supplement the volumes outlined above with a favorite book of their own, and others might want to take material from the daily newspaper. Evelyn Robinson's excellent collection of articles, *Readings About Children's Literature,* can be a useful aid in this process. Some will share a television program with the children and discuss it later. The importance of these materials is not so much their content but the parents' familiarity with them and their ability to stimulate thought. All this material, though part of the adult's daily fare, will be advanced to the child. With proper preparation and use of the inquiry method, it will help him to learn to think. He may not be able to digest it all at once or utilize it immediately, but it will make its impression and expand his mind.

There is a further ingredient which makes this process easier and infinitely more effective—the element of joy.

THE FUNCTION OF PLAY. A major factor in the Berle method is "harnessing the imagination," and the optimum time to do this is at play. Thus Berle used a question about a tennis court to teach geometry and some digging in the sand to make a point about Caesar's ramparts. All of this appeared quite casual; none of it was forced. All of it was fun.

A striking instance of Berle educating his children at play may be found in the names the children gave their dolls. Thus a doll named Mark Hanna (we might have

a John Lindsay today) led to a full discussion at the
dinner table about the exciting political campaign in
which Hanna had played a major part. Similarly, when
Cleopatra broke her head, she was suitably embalmed
in a compound of olive oil, cloves and cinnamon, and
was interred after a colorful procession based on an-
cient Egyptian lore. The children had fun playing with
these dolls and acting out these scenes. What is more,
they learned lessons they never forgot, and their minds
cried out for more.

Recently the "games curriculum" has taken hold at
various levels of education. As reported in Clark Abt's
Serious Games, this approach is successfully used with
adults in business schools and advanced military
courses. Also, it can be found at the secondary level in
such methods of instruction as the "British Empire
Game," where groups of students, on teams known as
"Southern Planters," "London Merchants" and the like,
compete for the accumulation of goods and profit and
come to some understanding of why the American
Revolution came about. Scientists have found that these
games create a favorable climate for education and that
the student motivated by the game will gain an increased enthusiasm for the subject matter.

In early youth these games may have an even more
profound effect on the learning experience. At this
stage, environment, including the artificial and highly
stimulating environment of the childhood game, can
give maximum effect to the genetic potential of the
child. What is this potential? It may be unlimited. Some
scientists estimate that we use only one tenth of the
potential of the brain, and others say we have tapped as
little as one percent of the brain's power.

Although Berle's initial objective was to increase knowledge, we see that the effect in his own family and on hundreds of other students was undoubtedly to increase intelligence. As he established new intellectual objectives, a more favorable climate for intelligent instruction and the elimination of waste in the early days of childhood, Berle insisted on the use of play to enhance "mental selfhood." Scientists are just beginning to understand that electrical and chemical impulses can have an effect on the brain and are part of the process by which the brain expands its own power. The element of joy, the interaction under pleasant circumstances of one human being with another, may create a chemical change in the DNA (deoxyribonucleic acid), which stores facts, and the RNA (ribonucleic acid), which transmits them among the brain's 10 billion neurons. Other scientists, who have come to regard the brain as a sort of natural computer (which is not without irony, since the computer was originally based on the operation of the mind), can sense some utility in the interdisciplinary approach to education which enables the brain's different memory cells to interlink factual inferences from one to another.

In *Education and Ecstasy,* George Leonard notes that "when joy is absent, the effectiveness of the learning process falls and falls until the human being is operating hesitantly, grudgingly, fearfully at only a tiny fraction of his potential." Whether the reason for this is electrical or chemical or cybernetic, it has become increasingly recognized as an ultimate truth. Yet our traditional educational system acts to suppress the element of joy, and, in the preschool years when this ingredient is so abundant in the child's life, parents

most often seem to ignore or, inadvertently, to destroy it.
Berle has shown how to use the power found in moments of joy and to extend their duration for a lifetime.

Walden Three

How does Berle work today? Perhaps the best way to
see Berle in action is to spend a week with a family that
employs the method. Below is a dramatization, based in
part on actual tapes of family experiences with the
Berle method and in part on some of the practices urged
by modern educational experimenters whose philosophy is consistent with Berle's. In many instances you
will recognize specific suggestions from the text or
elaborations on those suggestions.

Monday

*(It is seven o'clock in the evening on a Monday in April,
1972. The scene is a three-bedroom apartment in Building
Number Three of Walden Towers, a multibuilding, middle-
income housing development overlooking New York's East
River. As the doorbell rings Barbara Rogers, an attractive
woman in her late twenties, goes to answer it.)*
MOTHER *(opening door):* Hello, I'm Barbara Rogers. Please
   come in.
*(A short, bald, bespectacled man enters the apartment,
shaking hands briefly, then taking off his overcoat and hand-
ing it to Barbara.)*
OBSERVER: Good evening, Mrs. Rogers. I'm Dr. Smugg. Your
   husband told me to be here at seven o'clock *(he glances at
   the gold watch which he takes out of his vest pocket),* and
   that's exactly what time it is now.
*(At this point "Rodge" Rogers enters the room. He is a man
of medium height, dressed in an open-collared shirt, slacks
and loafers. He extends his hand to Dr. Smugg, they exchange
greetings and all three enter the library where three children*

are seated, engaged in animated conversation which stops as the adults enter the room.)

FATHER: Children, this is Dr. Smugg from the Bland Foundation. He will be dropping by every night this week to join us in some of our talks and games. Doctor, this is my daughter Maria. She is seven years old and is in the third grade at Saint Ann's School. This is my son, Burris. He is five years old and in kindergarten at Saint Ann's. And this young lady is my daughter Dewey. She is three years old and attends the local nursery school. The children all seem to be doing well in school and enjoy what they are doing. As for *our* educational background, I am a lawyer and Barbara has a bachelor's degree from Barnard, where she majored in philosophy. She is now a free-lance copywriter who works two days a week. How about some dinner?

(Everyone enters the dining room. Mother and Father are seated at the head and foot of the table, the two girls on one side and Burris and Dr. Smugg on the other. Food is being served and consumed throughout the following scene.)

FATHER: What did you do today, Dewey?

DEWEY: We spent most of the day at the playground. Sarah called me "chicken." What did she mean?

FATHER: What do you think, Burris?

BURRIS: She meant you were afraid.

DEWEY: I was not.

FATHER: Maria, where do you think the word came from?

MARIA: I guess chickens are supposed to be afraid.

FATHER: That may be it. Also it might come from the term "chicken-hearted," which means cowardly or timid.

DEWEY: I want to play "Witty Remark."

FATHER: All right, you begin.

DEWEY: *(turning to Maria):* You're chicken!

MARIA: That's a "fowl" remark.

MOTHER: I think it's for the birds.

BURRIS: Enough of this barnyard humor.

(Pause.)

FATHER: Your turn, Dr. Smugg.

DR. SMUGG: This seems somewhat flighty to me.

FATHER: Very good, Doctor.

DR. SMUGG: You have to go too now, Mr. Rogers.

FATHER: You mean you think I've taken advantage of the peck-
ing order?
(All groan.)
FATHER: Maria, what happened at your school today?
MARIA: We are still studying about different states. Mine is
Virginia. Today I learned that eight presidents came from
Virginia.
BURRIS: That's right. George Washington, James Madison,
Thomas Jefferson, James Monroe, William Henry Harrison,
John Tyler, Zachary Taylor, and Woodrow Wilson.
FATHER: Burris is very interested in presidents, Dr. Smugg.
Last year he was given a book with pictures and brief biog-
raphies of all the presidents. He can name the presidents in
order and tell you quite a bit about all of them. Which of the
Virginia presidents do you like best, Burris?
BURRIS: Washington was a great president, but I like Thomas
Jefferson the best.
FATHER: Why?
BURRIS: Because he could do so many things well. *(Speaking
rapidly.)* He had a machine that could write a lot of letters
at once and he built a beautiful home called Monticello. And
he wrote the Declaration of Independence. And he started
the University. And he bought Louisiana.
FATHER: Jefferson certainly could do a great many things. You
know, President Kennedy, when all of the Nobel Prize win-
ners had dinner at the White House, said it was the greatest
assemblage of talent ever to eat together at the White House
except on those evenings when Thomas Jefferson dined
alone.
DR. SMUGG: But he had one other distinction which no other
president had. Do you know what that was?
MARIA: Was it because he was Vice-President?
DR. SMUGG: No, other presidents did that. I'd better make my
point before I am asked too many questions. He was the only
president named Thomas.
FATHER: Very good, Doctor. I think that's right, isn't it, Burris?
BURRIS: Yes . . . except for Thomas Woodrow Wilson.
FATHER: I see that we are finished. You may be excused, children. Help your mother clear the table. Let me take you
through the apartment, Doctor.
*(The two men stroll through the apartment. As they pass
the kitchen, they hear an animated discussion on architec-
ture apparently inspired by Jefferson's design of Monticello.*

*In the girls' bedroom Dr. Smugg is introduced to a number of
dolls bearing names of statesmen, artists, historic figures. He
sees Maria's sewing machine and a half-completed finger
painting of Dewey's. Pictures hang on the walls in all of the
rooms. And all of them have a great many books. Games, balls
and stuffed animals are also seen everywhere. In Burris's
room, which is dominated by a card table piled with about
four layers of books, there is also a model hockey game on a
table. If there is a common theme, it is the presence of a large
number of books, many of them illustrated, in all of the
rooms, located so that they can be easily read or browsed. At
this point Dr. Smugg notes that he has to leave and proceeds
to the door, where, overcoat on, hat in hand, he speaks.)*

DR. SMUGG: I enjoyed the evening, Mr. Rogers, but I'm not sure
   what it proves.

FATHER: I'd like to get a grant from your foundation, Dr.
   Smugg, as you know. I believe that the simple games you
   have just seen and the atmosphere you have observed actually increase intelligence.

DR. SMUGG: Well, can't we test the children and see?

FATHER: They test very well, Doctor. But I don't think our
   standard intelligence test can measure the whole thing.
   What I want is a grant to conduct a longitudinal study so that
   these children and others taught by the Berle method can be
   observed throughout their lives, as the Berle family was. At
   the very least, as you have seen, they have accumulated a
   significant amount of knowledge and vocabularies that enable them to learn more than children who are not so well
   equipped to receive the knowledge about them. Well, keep
   an open mind, Doctor. See you tomorrow night.

Tuesday

*(The scene is the living room of the Rogers' home. The
family and Dr. Smugg are gathered around the television set.
A documentary entitled* Lost Atlantis, *reviewing various
American civilizations of centuries past, has just concluded.
As Barbara turns off the set, Dewey speaks.)*

DEWEY: What happened to those Indians, Mommy?

MOTHER: Well, they told us some of the things during the
   show. Can you recall some of them, Maria?

MARIA: Yes, the Spaniards killed the Aztecs in Mexico, and
   they also attacked the Incas in Peru.

BURRIS: And the Olmecs and Mayans just seemed to disappear.

They may have been warring among themselves or it may have been an epidemic of some kind.

DEWEY: But aren't some of them alive today?

MOTHER: A number of descendents of the various civilizations we saw are still alive, but there is a very different way in which they live today. Some of the people lived but their civilizations died. They now form parts of a different culture.

MARIA: I thought you said the other night that a culture was something where germs grow.

MOTHER: The word can mean that, too. When I just used it I meant a civilization or a system of customs and characteristics which have developed among a people. When we used the word the other day, we were talking about how you can grow bacteria on certain types of food. *(At this point Barbara refers to a dictionary.)* Actually the word comes from the Latin word *colere,* which means to till or cultivate the soil. So it's the same word, Maria, but it has two different meanings, and, as you can see, the meanings are related. All right, get ready for bed now. Then Dr. Smugg will come in to hear "The Story."

(The scene now changes to the girls' bedroom. All three children are in their pajamas and bathrobes. The girls are on their bunk beds, and Burris is sitting in a small chair across the room.)

FATHER: Doctor, this is a story entitled "The Adventures of Three Children," which has been going on for over a year now. We add a little bit each night that we do this, at least twice a week. Dewey, why don't you begin tonight?

DEWEY: The children got up very early and started walking. They walked and walked and walked and walked. They found this big hill and they walked up the hill and they were scared.

FATHER: All right, Burris, take it from there.

BURRIS: Nobody knew who put the hill there, but there was something scary about it. On the top of the hill they found some arrowheads and a bowl. This hill was built by Indians millions of years ago.

FATHER: More likely hundreds of years ago, Burris, if you are thinking of the hills we saw on television tonight. Maria, why don't you conclude this chapter?

MARIA: The bowl they found was covered with red *(she pauses dramatically)*, and this was blood! These Indians had a wonderful culture *(she looks briefly at Mother)*, but when the leaders of the tribe became too powerful they called themselves gods and they stood on the hill and killed other people in the tribe. But soon the other people didn't like this and they threw out the leaders. Then a lot of the men in the country started killing one another, and all that was left was the big mound and the arrowheads and the bowl that was covered in red.

Wednesday

On Wednesday Dr. Smugg arrived after dinner. He witnessed a game of charades and a three-act play in which each child was responsible for an act. It was up to the child who would participate in his or her portion of the play. These vignettes were frequently elaborations on old jokes or vaudeville routines such as this one:

BURRIS *(holding a toy telephone to his ear)*: Ring, ring. *(He picks up the phone and says the following with a different emphasis each time.)* You don't say, you don't say, you don't say, you don't say, you don't say.
FATHER: Who was it?
BURRIS: He didn't say.

The girls' portion of the play was done entirely on Maria's tape recorder. It featured a number of singing commercials based on products the family used in the home or that the girls had seen at the local market. At the end of the evening the whole family gathered around the piano and sang a number of songs.

Dr. Smugg raised the question of how the children did on various achievement tests and how the activities he had witnessed could possibly help them on these tests. Rodge replied that they did exceptionally well on tests (even Dewey had to take one in order to get into nursery school), but that tests were really inadequate to capture

what was being achieved in these sessions. First of all,
many things were *not* being done: the dull, the turgid,
the repetitive, the bland, the incorrect was consciously
being eliminated from the daily fare the children received. If the quantity of time that parents and children
spent with each other was not increased, the quality
was. The yield, Rodge maintained, was better mental
organization and increased intelligence. The children
were learning to think. While standard tests could measure this, the real guide would be a longitudinal study
that took them through their lives and compared them
to some control group. The results with the Berle children had been striking. At the short range, of course,
Rodge could point to certain spectacular demonstra-
tions of knowledge which the small children had mastered. The television documentary on lost cultures was
tucked into a mental framework begun originally in a
discussion of biology a number of days before. These
pieces of knowledge would tend to reinforce each other
and create a receptivity for further knowledge. Similarly, Burris's knowledge of the presidents would be
useful to him throughout school as a framework within
which to understand American history and governmental forms everywhere. Also, because the positive
accomplishments of the presidents were emphasized in
the short biographies he read, it would create in his
young mind high standards which he would seek to
achieve. There was no attempt to structure the exact
nature of the knowledge the children would receive.
Indeed, no specific games or activities were set down for
any specific nights. There was something pleasantly
random about the activity.

Dr. Smugg was beginning to believe. Rodge pointed

out that these activities, infused with a heavy element of joy which seemed to make them more productive and yield a significant mental expansion, were much like exercise for the body, where the end was not the exercise itself but the results that would be achieved and would prepare the body for other activities.

As they parted Wednesday night, Dr. Smugg asked Rodge a question that had been troubling him for some time. He noted that he was impressed with what was happening at Walden Three, but pointed out that the Rogers had many distinct advantages, some of them genetic, some environmental. They were well-educated and economically well off. Would the system work in a home that did not have these advantages? Without elaborating at any length, Rodge said that this was a legitimate question which he would try to answer the following night.

Thursday

(The basement at Walden Three was unlike the other floors. Instead of recessed fluorescent lighting, there were naked light bulbs. The cinderblock walls were unplastered and unpainted. There were large rooms for storing things and keeping bicycles and wagons. There was only one apartment on the basement floor. The nameplate on the door read "Mrs. George Johnson, Superintendent."

As the scene opens, Rodge and Dr. Smugg have entered the two-room apartment. A large room includes a kitchenette and a convertible sofa which forms a bed for George, Jr., age seven. The door to Mrs. Johnson's bedroom is at one side. The walls of the main room are covered with photographs and paintings. Most of these are outdoor scenes, but there are also portraits of Robert F. Kennedy and Martin Luther King. As in the Rogers' apartment, books abound. Although there is no bound set of encyclopedia, there is a 1972 world almanac; a paperback dictionary; random paperbacks, such as Guiness Book of

Records *and* The Autobiography of Malcolm X; *and a number of children's classics, such as* Alice in Wonderland *and* Treasure Island. The School in the Home *and the Holy Bible are prominently displayed. Presently, George, Jr., a handsome black youngster, comes over and shakes hands with Rodge Rogers.)*

GEORGE: How about a game of "Dog-Bark-Tree," Mr. Rogers?

ROGERS: That sounds fine, George. You and your mother and I can play, and Dr. Smugg can watch. As you'll see, Doctor, this is a word-series game where the first and second words have a relationship, as do the second and third words, but the first and third are unrelated. Puns are allowed, by the way.

ROGERS: Travel.

MOTHER: Trip.

GEORGE: Fall.

ROGERS: Hair.

MOTHER: Rabbit.

GEORGE: Hole.

ROGERS: Pie.

MOTHER: Square (as in π^2).

GEORGE: Hippie.

ROGERS: Girdle.

MOTHER: Sheath.

ROGERS: Knife.

GEORGE: Night.

ROGERS: Star.

MOTHER: Hollywood.

GEORGE: Tree (you know—wood, tree, hee! hee!).

ROGERS: Bark.

MOTHER: Dog.

ALL *(cheering):* Yea!

ROGERS: That was a stimulating game, George.

GEORGE: Thanks. I have an antiphon for you: *read.*

ROGERS: Doctor, "antiphon" is a word we made up to describe a class of words that have the same spelling but different sounds. Thus a word that is spelled *r-e-a-d* can be pronounced two ways, as in: I intend to *read* the book and I have *read* the book. That's a good one, George.

DR. SMUGG: Mrs. Johnson, do you find this program helpful?

MRS. JOHNSON: George is the smartest boy in his class in third grade at PS 18, and he is also interested in a lot of things he is not taught at school. Every night I read out of a textbook of black history that was prepared for a college course, and he can tell you a great deal about that area. Now let me answer a question that you are too polite to ask. Rodge and Barbara have both been to college. I haven't. My husband left the family a number of years ago and we don't have the money to buy all the books that the Rogers have. But I have seen great results in what I am doing, and I find that it makes my life and George's more interesting. So even though I may not be able to do quite the same job that Rodge and Barbara do, it's worthwhile. And there's one other point that I think clinches the argument.

DR. SMUGG: What's that, Mrs. Johnson?

MRS. JOHNSON: It's better than it was, Doctor, much, much better than it was.

Friday

(The scene is Madison Square Garden. The Rogers family, George Johnson, Jr., and Dr. Smugg are all watching a rodeo that has been going on for some time. They have been engaged in lively conversation and as we listen in, we hear:)

MARIA: Do they have rodeos in other parts of the country, Daddy?

FATHER: Oh yes. Matter of fact, most of them are out West. The word *rodeo* is a Spanish word meaning "round-up," and rodeos started in the West over a hundred years ago as a celebration after the work of round-up had been done. But today a lot of cowboys compete in rodeos as a profession, earning their living through the prizes that are awarded.

BURRIS: How much money do they get, Daddy?

FATHER: Well, they win a cash prize for each event, such as bronc riding, bull riding, and the one you see down there now, calf-roping. The cowboy who has won the most money at the end of the year is the world champion all-round cowboy. Prizes total more than three million dollars a year.

DR. SMUGG: Well, I'm impressed. I didn't know that you knew so much about rodeos, Rodge.

FATHER: To be honest, I didn't until just before we left, Doc. But a little preparation makes the event more interesting, so before we came out I took a minute portion— *(at that point Maria and George, Jr., look at each other and shout together:)*

MARIA and GEORGE, JR. An antiphon—that's an antiphon!

FATHER: So it is, *minute.* Good work. Preparation doesn't take much time. For example, I've done some reading on the Pennsylvania Dutch country for the trip that we plan to take this weekend. Maria can't go because some of her friends at school have asked her over. The other two children will come, and George is going to join us. Understand, Doc, that these occasions are not exhaustive lectures by me. They just fertilize the mind, as Berle would say. The kids do the rest. They develop knowledge which you wouldn't believe in some of these areas.

DR. SMUGG: Rodge, I don't mind saying I'm impressed. These are the liveliest, most interesting children I have seen in some time. I think you should have a foundation grant to let the world see how lives can be enhanced and intelligence expanded. At the very least we should show everybody how much fun family life can be. But right now I've got a "witty remark." *(Dr. Smugg holds up a cellophane-wrapped sandwich which he had purchased at the concession on the way into the rodeo.)* Why are you children like a part of this sandwich? *(Silence.)* Because you are "wry bred." *(Polite laughter. All groan.)*

A Word in Conclusion

Centering largely on family occasions such as mealtime, the Berle method takes less than an hour a day to implement. This seems like a small time commitment for such an immense task, until one realizes that foreign languages and advanced sciences are generally taught in fifty-minute daily classes. Also, the parent's role is, in Berle's scheme of things, not supposed to take a great deal of time. The parent stimulates; the child responds and develops. It is the quality of the time that the two spend together which is changed under the Berle method. The initial change in the relationship must be a new state of awareness in the parent.

The Office of Child Development has promulgated guidelines for the Home Start Program, which point out a basic fact that many professional educators have ignored: "The parent is the first and most influential educator and 'enabler' of his or her own children." Much of *The School in the Home* is devoted to "eliminating waste" that frequently occurs in the typical parent-child relationship. The parent cannot avoid being a teacher of his child. If he ignores the opportunity, bad habits and dullness will gain hold. If he exploits the occasion, he can increase his child's knowledge and intelligence. There is no middle course.

A great deal of the literature in the educational field is confusing to parents. Some very exciting ideas, such as the use of Cuisenaire rods in teaching principles of mathematics to small children and the modern math approach in teaching older children, are simply too complex for most parents to absorb. Even experienced teachers need detailed personal instruction in learning how to use these methods. The literature is made even more confusing by frequently contradictory points of view, stated with absolute certainty, by opposing schools and the rapidity with which new ideas are adopted and then discarded. In this country and this century we have seen significant elements in the educational establishment endorse John Dewey and Maria Montessori, reject them with certainty, and then endorse them again with enthusiasm. In the last two decades we have seen the emergence of Sputnik change the emphasis in American education to concentrated coverage of scientific subjects, and then we have seen the focus shift back to development of the "whole child." Within the past ten years teaching machines came quickly and dramatically into vogue; now it is realized that they are not the total solution they were once thought to be.

In the midst of the eternal debate on educational theory, a compelling fact should be borne in mind: the Berle method works. The author gives numerous examples of successful teaching in his writings, and his family presents the best evidence. The method creates a framework of self-organization and an intellectual climate in the home which can foster brilliant creative thought. It can lead to a rare combination of intellectual curiosity and practical action. It does not require large staffs, expensive buildings or elaborate equipment. Dr. Berle, with deceptive simplicity, has provided a way in which parental love and interest can be used to make children more happy and productive human beings.

INDEX